ॐ ✡ ♆ ☪ ✵ 🧘 ॐ ⸰ ☯ ✝

FLOWERS FACING THE SUN

By: Ben B. Boothe

FLOWERS FACING THE SUN
The Emerging Religion of the Global Generation

By Ben B. Boothe

In the springtime, the pasture at the Boothe Ranch in Texas is ablaze with thousands of flowers. Golden yellow blooms, a dozen different shades of blue, purple & pink flowers as diverse as one can imagine. A riot of shapes of tiny cups, stars, some with five petals, some with thirteen petals, each one unique. In the mornings they all bow to the East, each independent, but all together. There is a common energy commanding all. They bow as in holy reverence, flowers seeking the sun...

This book describes a new perspective of exciting and revolutionary religious attitudes sweeping the world of the global generation. It is written by one who has circled the globe and counts friends from every spectrum of the religious world. Not since Joseph Campbell has anyone so well captured the religious heart of the "global generation."

UNICORN PRESS U.S.A.
Fort Worth, Texas

2

Other books and symposiums by Ben Boothe:

Confessions of a Banker

To Be or Not to Be an SOB (a reaffirmation of business ethics)

Grandpa's Hat (a common sense guide to life)

How to Bullet Proof Your Real Estate Portfolio with FIRREA

A Banker Tells You How to Borrow All the Money You'll Ever Need

A Quiet Place Poems by Paulette Boothe

Symposiums:
1. Winners and Losers in the New Global Economy
2. Restructuring of Financial Systems during times of Crisis
3. Ethics in Business and Culture
4. Grandpa's Hat, A Common Sense Guide to Life

UNICORN PRESS U.S.A.
Fort Worth, Texas

9800 Verna Trail N. Ft. Worth, Texas 76108 U.S.A.
Phone: 817-246-6262 benboothe@compuserve.com
www.benboothe.com

Flowers Facing the Sun (the emerging religion of the global generation)
Copyright 2003 First Edition by Ben Boothe

ISBN # 1-878162-07-1

Cover design by Dale Berkebile Illustration Design

Daleberkebile.com

Thanks and Dedicated to: Friends who contributed to the thought process, many unnamed but with the appreciation that no endeavor in life is achieved without help of others.

Special thanks to:
Waymon Featherston and Marvin Carlile who taught me grace and social responsibility.

My father, who gave me life and a desire to do good.

My mother Pauletta Daniels who kept me alive and showed me how to laugh.

My wife Paulette Boothe for her encouragement.

Bob Collier of Post, Texas, who taught lessons of love.
Lloyd Weaver, who taught lessons of intellect.

R.C. Leonard, who taught me multicultural breadth.

Tsering Migyur and Woser Chodon, in India who introduced me to Tibetan culture, its emphasis on compassion and the joy of being a part of their family.

Demir Yener, with the World Bank & USAID who gave me confidence and tools to circle the globe.

Richard Hall, who encouraged me to write this book
Claire Villiareal, Kit Jones, Nina Watson and Brenda Knowles who helped edit this book.

My two sons, Ben Boothe II, a lawyer, for his insights and Ethan Boothe, a businessman, who understands positive energy & love.

Ram Katri, a banker in Nepal for his insights world peace and development and for introducing me to leaders of Nepal.

Deepak Nirula, hotel owner on Connaught Place in New Delhi, for his perspective on world political trends.

Murl Richardson, Texas engineer and rancher, who encouraged me "not" to get a job causing me to find inner resources for success.

Ralph Hall, U.S. Congress, for his enduring friendship, and for opening doors for me throughout the world.

Mandeep Kaur, U.S. State Department, Delhi, for putting me before leaders of India and inspiring me with her encouragement and support.

To many others who have provided kindness, love and encouragement. We are all a part of each other through the love and ideas that we share.

CHAPTERS

INTRODUCTION

ॐ ✡ ♉ ☪ ❖ 🧘 ॐ ∽ ☯ ✝

FLOWERS FACING THE SUN
(The Emerging Religion of the Global Generation)

In the springtime, the pasture at the Boothe Ranch in Texas is ablaze with thousands of flowers. Golden yellow blooms, interspersed with dozen different blues, purple & pink flowers as diverse as one can imagine. A riot of shapes of tiny cups, stars, some with five petals, some thirteen petals, but each one unique. In the mornings they all bow to the east, each independent but all together; there is a common energy commanding all. They bow as in holy reverence, flowers seeking the sun...

Prak Samnang was 24 years old when I met her in Phenom Phen. She was working as a waitress at the Inter-Continental Hotel and served my breakfast every morning. It seemed that everyone was young in Cambodia in 1998 because an entire generation of Cambodians had been killed by war or died in the camps of Pol Pot. Prak was working two jobs trying to survive. Her father had been a respected businessman. "One day during Pol Pot, soldiers came to our house and took him away. We never saw him again" she said. She lost most of her family to war. It seemed that every family of Cambodia had lost someone during those terrible years of 1965 through 1985. Out of a population of seven million people over a million five hundred thousand were killed. The Pol Pot regime became so strict that if

7

a person wore reading glasses, he was labeled as "one the educated class" and sent to the death camps.

Prak went to night classes to learn computers and began e-mailing people around the globe. When foreign visitors would speak, she asked them about their culture and shared stories about her background. She had an insatiable curiosity. One day she said something that surprised me. "My Grandparents were Buddhist. My parents were Buddhist and I was raised Buddhist too. But I see now that there are other good people in the world." I said: "Even Christians?" She smiled and said: "Even Christians from Texas." Prak Samnang was changing from sociocentric to worldcentric. She had learned that her group was not the only group in the world.

Something new is sweeping the world. In my travels around the globe I have observed it among members of every world religion. The educated global set or what I call the 'connected generation', connected by communication systems, education and travel experience, has embraced this philosophy by the millions. It represents a fundamental change in attitudes toward religion and humanity's quest for enlightenment. It has a religious language not based in negative judgments but in a deeper study of what we all have in common. It represents a broader way to deal with inconsistencies and shortcomings of institutionalized religion. It will have enormous impacts upon the way we worship and interact as nations, institutions and as individuals. It is the emerging religion of the global generation. It takes people from an egocentric, sociocentric place to a worldcentric perspective. It begins with the most basic of questions.

WHO ARE YOU? WHAT ARE WE?

Can you describe yourself in fifty words or less?

Do you have a clear idea of what or who you are at the most basic level?

Are you a soccer fan, a football fan, lover of poetry, scholar, businessman, manager, teacher, cab driver, student, professor? Some of these suggest more about what you do than whom and what you are.

Are you an American, Indian, German, Pakistani, Canadian, Mexican, Iraqi, Nepali, Mongolian, Tibetan? These tell me where you were born but not much about who you are.

Who? What?

These questions refined down to the most fundamental level can lead us to areas that we have in common, *the areas where we are one!*

We are not just flesh and bone, not just electronic impulses, not just chemical compounds, not just animals who eat, sleep, and die. We are something more. The consciousness that gives us love, a sense of ethics and that inspired area, that special time when we are in the "zone" is within our reach. You and I at the most fundamental level are spiritual beings.

Only with this basic understanding can we then describe who we are. A description such as a Christian, Hindu, Buddhist, Muslim, or Atheist may be inadequate or divisive. That type of description merely defines the intellectual and spiritual path you have chosen to organize your spiritual thoughts. Perhaps it describes some other person's definitions of good or evil. *Your* path, the path that you hope leads to happiness, peace, enlightenment, goodness and love may not be fully defined by rigid institutional mandates. Is it possible that you disagree with some aspects of some ideologies that are accepted in your culture and yet find things in other ideologies that are helpful to you? Can we accept the good in all religions without being judgmental and find spiritual insights?

Perhaps descriptions of our nationality, occupation, title, geography and autobiography can help define some things about us. But do these tell who you and I are? Who and what we are impacts everything and everything colors who we are.

Go one step deeper now. Define the inner qualities that define you. Perhaps you will say: "I am a seeker, often alone in a journey to find happiness. I've done my share of good and bad. Ultimately, I believe we are all alone in the most basic aspects of life and death, but I enjoy the love and affection of others here and now. I love people. I am a good friend. I am scared sometimes, and sometimes in awe of nature, beauty, love, music, poetry and ideas. Let me tell you about the moments when I am 'in the zone' and have 'found my joy'." It is at those times that we feel like we are significant or have made a difference through our existence."

In these definitions we find commonality. *We* are *one!* We see that we are spiritual beings. We are brothers and sisters on the most basic level. We need to see beyond definitions such as what church or temple we attend, what intellectual system we subscribe to, what club or institution we are members of. Those may be intellectual prisons, or they may be doors or windows, that lead to something better. But they do not absolutely determine what we are or who we are. *You and I are spiritual beings. We are one!*

We are fragile humans, tiny in this infinite universe, possessed with a seed of power that can make our love, our ideas, our inspired moments shine and be seen throughout creation! This assumes that we can open and touch the spiritual button that frees our power and places us in total focus, totally in the "zone". We are consciousness trapped in a flexible body of blood, skin, and hair and within this body is a person wandering through the universe always noting the seeming random, unfair, almost tragic events of life while wondering, what it all means? Is it a random joke, a prank? Is it something greater and ultimately filled with spiritual meaning? Then we catch a taste, sound, or scent of the "inspired." We may see a saint saving the lives of children or ministering to the hungry, comforting widows, being a loving friend or a respectful lover. Then we begin to believe that there is meaning to it all.

This week I read a story about an American photojournalist who photographed an Iraqi child whose body was riddled with shrapnel from an American bomb. The photojournalist devoted himself to helping that child. He was driven by an inspired compassion in the face of the terror of war. Such beauty, such inspirational power can not exist in a totally random universe. When you realize that you are a friend, comforter, teacher, that encourager, you begin to see the core of who you are. You have started the process of releasing the positive energy that is within your soul.

We, in this world of fast and inexpensive communication with the ability to travel the world quickly and inexpensively might be called the connected generation. Many of this "global" generation are going beyond superficial acceptance of established institutional barriers to unity and intellectual progress. Many are seeing perspectives deeper than those thrust upon us by politicians and the media. Many are delving into basic issues of enlightenment that turn us to the most elemental and universal spiritual journey. It is a language of commonality, not hostility. A language that understands the central basic issues of our existence. Who and what we are. When we understand how we are similar, then we can focus on ideas that we can unite on.

It seems that the nature of some people is to divide, to judge or to create circles of exclusion. Those people create circles within circles, defining "us" as the "in" group and everyone else "out." With these barriers, some justify all kinds of mischief and cruelty. The ultimate goal of the spiritual being is to learn to see what unites us, to learn to see through all of the barriers and social and cultural walls that have been erected over thousands of years, and see the "who and what" with clarity. Our purpose is not to judge or to condemn but to embrace and explore the spiritual being in each other. Then we can strive together to let the spiritual being within each of us bond and interact as it comes out and shines in the world. Great power is unleashed when this occurs. Much of the language of institutional religion tends to speak in differences. It tends to define people and groups by how they are wrong. Religious and political language tends to insist on telling us which group we can accept or reject. The global generation has another emphasis. It is not the language of judgment or exclusion. It is a language that says "We accept the good in all religions" or more specifically, "we accept the beauty of all philosophies." It is a language that points out that no religion, no person, no political party and no ideology has exhausted all of the possibilities of truth, or perfection.

I know that as a living spirit, you are a beautiful person. As a member of the global generation, your identity exists with a world centric global awareness as a part of the circle of all humanity. Let us find each other. Let our spirits blend. We are the connected children of the global generation. While we have political and institutional loyalties, at the core we are something more than just Americans, Indians, Iraqis, or Germans. We are something more than Baptists, Buddhists, Hindus or Christians. We are not this body but rather we are spiritual energy, spiritual beings. We are all related and of one source. This is God-work that we are about. Let's get on with it!

CHAPTER ONE

ॐ ✡ ♆ ☪ ✳ 🧘 ॐ ∞ ☯ ✝

THE BASIS FOR THE EMERGING RELIGION OF THE GLOBAL GENERATION

*"I am convinced that it is possible to be a person of faith with integrity. It is possible to be Christian, Hindu, Jew, Muslim, and Buddhist and at the same time recognize that one's own experience of God does not exhaust all of the possibilities. A constructive outlook of religious pluralism can take us beyond simple tolerance of others; it can provide a framework for celebrating diversity and embracing it as source of strength." Charles Kimball **When Religion Becomes Evil***

One evening in Kathmandu, I was sitting in an outdoor restaurant with two brothers of the Sakya family. As natives of Nepal, their traditional Buddhist culture dictates that every son should devote a period of his life as a Buddhist monk before continuing his career. Each of these brothers had complied but it was apparent that these young men had a different religious perspective than their parents. As we visited, they shared their love and respect for their religious heritage but they also had developed a much broader view. One told me: "My mother goes to the temple and prays every day. She is a devoted Buddhist but my brothers and I respect Christians, Muslims, and Hindus and can see the deeper ethos, the deeper meaning common to all religions." These Buddhist brothers were able to embrace me, an

American of Christian culture, as their spiritual brother.

These young men are educated, technically competent, internet active, and communicate with people throughout the world. We sat together under the stars of Nepal that night and shared our dreams. We spoke of how special it would be to create a universal symbol to recognize and revere all religions. Ujaya and his brother spoke of what a symbol could look like. One idea was a hand with a cross, a Tibetan and Hindu "OM", a Jewish star, a Muslim crescent moon, all in the palm of a large hand, suggested the "maker". We visualized a mountain with many trails to the top with all of the great religious symbols at the crest. It was joyful to imagine and consider a symbol suggesting the beauty of all religions.

That night under the stars of Nepal, we shared experiences that we had each enjoyed with our acquaintances and contacts around the world. We then began to understand and define phenomena that we had all noticed. We identified a massive acceptance among the "connected generation" of a new religious concept throughout the world. Indeed the movement is spreading globally even though it is unnamed and not institutionalized.

Traditional religious sects are not being embraced by the new global generation as the sole landlords of religious faith. In some cases the sects are gradually shrinking and being replaced, but they don't realize it. Their membership is growing older and the youth are not staying with them. As their members die, so do their institutions. This is not a conspiracy. It is not happening because of evangelism, force, intimidation, or persecution. The change is natural and not motivated by money or any specific organized group. It is simply a cultural event of global proportions. It is powerful and cataclysmic to some established religious institutions. They are finding that as their membership declines, their resources, funds and power declines. They are finding themselves in a spiral of decline that they cannot reverse. Those who have traditionally thrived on political power associated with religious organizations find it the most cataclysmic for their personal power is threatened. Some feel the growing gnawing pain of realization that something is wrong, something is drifting away and they are right! It is their power and security. Some will use all means, even violence, to protect their power. They will define it as protecting "our" religion but they too, will be overwhelmed by the wave of change. It is a "sea change" that is moving in like a tide, slow, relentless, unstoppable.

The new world religion is made up of young and old, educated and connected. They are often people who have studied and sometimes traveled the world. They have sought and found beauty and direction and common goals of religions all over the world. They see the core roots and truths of religious symbolism. They understand rituals, myths, art, music, and teachings as doorways, windows to greater truth, and to a greater reality...to a greater connection with what some people call "God" "Shiva" Nirvana" "Allah" "Jaweh" "Buddha," "enlightenment," and the ultimate reality and energy that is the source, goal, and destination of all religions.

These people, the "New Global Citizens" are such because they are interested in core truth and have the intelligence and ability to seek it out. National or political barriers and borders have less relevance to them. These Citizens first observe the common ethos of religions.

I am such a Citizen of the world. I have worshipped with Sikhs in India, Buddhists in Tibet, Hindus at Banaras (Varanasi) and Nepal, Jews in America, Hare Krishna's in India and the United States, Catholics, Protestants, and have sat with and exchanged ideas with representatives of many other religions. My conclusion, in large measure, refines all of these religious systems down to their core values. It is the core values that are important because they define religions. The core values define what their leaders and founders are trying to say. Almost without exception, the founders of these religions tried to avoid the symbolic, political and organizational trappings that always seem to evolve after the religious visionary has died or passed from the scene.

One of the basic core values is that people throughout the world have some kind of religious impulse to better themselves, to organize thought systems into systems of logic, beauty, hope and promise. With that understanding, we can see that we are all taking paths of enlightenment. Some of the paths are parallel; some very different. But we are all ascending the same mountain of personal and spiritual development. The mountain is so vast that sometimes we cannot see the others or their path. The mountain looks different from different perspectives and is so large that no one person or group can see or fully grasp its entirety. But we are all seeking to scale the summit to improve ourselves intellectually and spiritually and to connect with the enlightenment that we hope for, that we know, that we trust is at the summit. For some, the journey is as important as the goal, as the destination for the journey (one step at time) is where we are living, experiencing, learning and developing. We are "alive" as long as we are on the journey. The journey may define a life, a people, a philosophy, even though the goal may not always be attained.

Kesava Bhart Daj (K.B.) is a monk of the Gauidya Vaisnava Sampradaya religion of India. He told me about a concept that was written down over 1000 years ago in the Bhavisya Purana. That work predicted that there will be an amalgamation of all religions, greater religious tolerance, greater religious unity, and adoption of global "core" religious ethical values. This global generation is the fulfillment of that prophecy.

What are these "core" values? They are the same values that almost all religions teach, but many are just discovering that they share similar, sometimes identical values with philosophies far away in distance and in culture. They realize that in their quest for enlightenment, that they are not the only ones to have found core truths shared by millions on this globe. What are some of the core values in the value system for the religion of the citizens of the new global order?

Kindness, compassion, honesty, generosity, love, hospitality, modesty, cleanliness, self control, cultivation of spiritual values, search for knowledge and truth, non violence, forgiveness, vigor, freedom from envy, jealousy and destructive pride.

"K.B." sees this "amalgamation" happening in India today, especially among the younger generation. "They aren't tied to their parent's pre-judgments", he says.

Loren Streit, a college student from Dallas Texas is a good example. On an airplane from Dallas to L.A., to visit her boyfriend, she told me; "Our generation communicates with people world wide. I was raised as an Episcopalian, but I can accept and appreciate a Hindu, Moslem or Buddhist. The key is, "Are they good people, do they follow the universal core values that all of our religions have in common?"

A Sikh invited me to his temple worship service in Mumbai, India. As we walked to the front door he whispered "Out of reverence, take off your shoes, and cover your head". We entered and sat on the floor as a group of musicians played their drums and stringed instruments in an exotic Indian tempo. The music went on for a long time. It seemed to flow through us. I began to meditate and think of spiritual things. Then, one by one, the worshippers walked to the front and prostrated themselves before the cleric. We then adjourned to the basement community room where the members happily prepared a meal for everyone. It reminded me of going to church in the mountains of New Mexico as a child, listening to the music, going forward for communion, and then having a pot luck dinner afterward. As a child I was learning reverence, meditation, hospitality, the joy of fellowship, and kindness. The only difference from the Sikh experience and the experience of my church as a child seemed to be that in the Sikh temple, the women wore veils and the men covered their heads and took off their shoes. The women in the mountains of New Mexico wore veils as well, but they were connected to big flowery hats. The food in New Mexico was fried chicken, instead of steamed rice and sweet fruits. But what were they teaching? Why these meetings? "Love your neighbors, eat and worship together to learn generosity and sharing. Be friends, don't lie, steal or harm one another. Be compassionate and loving." The ethos? The same!

Brishan Khatri is from Nepal. He visited the United States in the late 1990s, got a degree, and now has a high tech computer job in Austin, Texas. He was reared in a Hindu family. His mother is very orthodox, prays daily and goes to temple. His father, Ram Khatri, is a banking executive, a leader of the sect. They are building a new temple in Kathmandu, Nepal. His father is also the publisher of a magazine that interviews world leaders and thinkers. But here is the irony. As the son has been exposed to those of other cultures, his religious views have broadened. He can now accept Christians, Jews, Hindus and Buddhists as fellow seekers of truth, blessed by a divine spirit. His father has also become more educated because of extensive global contact through his business and publishing contacts. His father, although one of the leaders of his religious group in Nepal, has come to be able to accept and work with people of other faiths. As this father and son have broadened their knowledge and contacts around the world, they have broadened their faith, their fellowship, and their tolerance. They now are part of a "Global family" of enlightened seekers. The "ethics of nearly all religions are the same" Brishan told me on a visit to our ranch in Texas.

Shea Parker, a 23 year old woman was a student of a conservative Christian school called Criswell College in Texas when I met her. She told me that one of her professors believed that their religious denomination had the truth. I answered: "Oh I'm so glad; I've looked so hard for someone who has all of the truth." She stopped me and said: "Oh, we don't have all of the truth!" "I've searched the entire globe for someone, some group that had it all." I said. I told her about my young Buddhist friends in Nepal and asked her how she would respond to them if they were sitting at our table. "Oh, I love people, I wouldn't judge them. I would consider them my brothers." she said, exemplifying the attitudes of this generation. When we are simplistic in our new found faiths, we tend to make circles, indicating that everyone in that circle "has the truth." We can accept them. But as we grow and experience more, our circles tend to be redrawn larger and more inclusive. The more depth oriented, the more grace oriented, the more love oriented we become, the less judgmental we become. Then a magnificent realization comes upon us. We are not intended to be in the circle drawing business, the business of judging others.

Murl Richardson is a Texas rancher and an engineer. He has worked all over the world developing oil platforms and oil-fields for governments. One day he approached a high level Chinese leader to request that China designate Murl's church as an "approved" religion in China. The Chinese government official replied: "We have over 269 applications from churches, all claiming to be Christians. You go back to America and when you can get all 269 of them to agree on one central message then I will approve your application. We don't want 269 denominations all teaching different messages in the name of Christianity confusing our people in China." Murl came back realizing that the Chinese government had a point. In the United States, there are hundreds of different religious denominations and hundreds more sub-sects that have different viewpoints. The Baptist Church has the "Southern

Baptists," the "Free Will Baptists," the "Northern Baptists," the "Primitive Baptists" and over 120 different types of Baptist churches and that is only *one* denomination. Consider the hundreds, perhaps thousands of other groups in America.

Which one has all of the truth? Which one has exhausted all spiritual possibilities and has all truth properly understood? Then broaden the question to denominations. Which brand of Christianity of all churches in America has all of the truth? Then let's narrow the question. Is there even one person who has all of the truth? Then look to other nations. Africa has over 900 different religions. Which one has exhausted all spiritual potentialities of the truth? India has over 30,000 different religions. Does one of them have it completely right? Tibet, Nepal, Thailand and Cambodia all have different types of Buddhism.

Which one has it perfectly right? Israel has one religion, but perhaps 150 different types of that religion exist with varied opinions and interpretations all with different teachings. Which one has all of the truth? Islam has hundreds of sub-sects, and we still haven't found one that is perfect. Of course there are some who will be more comfortable in the structure of their traditional institutional religion. Where ever a person finds his song we give our blessings and our acceptance. For the world has 50,000 or more religions, all have good spiritual seekers, diverse, yet beautiful, like flowers facing the sun. None have exhausted every possibility of truth.

But with the realization of so much diversity it becomes obvious that the circle drawing business that many participate in is essentially an endeavor of judging others and keeping others out. Shea Parker is right that we shouldn't be involved in drawing exclusive circles. The key comes from something her father suggested. He said that global citizens are learning to treat all people, as diverse as humanity is, with dignity, acceptance, love and respect. This assumes the basic revelation that that they too are flowers facing the sun.

THAT is what the children of the new order can see and understand. Whether you call the primary deity or saint of your religion God, Shiva or Krishna, if they all give you similar suggestions, isn't it the same mountain we are climbing?

Notice the common suggestions from all of the major religions:

- Love one another
- Be good, kind and generous
- Don't kill
- Don't steal
- Don't judge others
- Take care of the poor
- Support widows and orphans
- Respect truth and virtue
- Try to grow spiritually and intellectually
- Learn to love nature
- Respect your fellow man and treat them as you would want to be treated
- Live with compassion

Diana Eck was awarded the National Humanities Medal in 1998 by President Clinton because of her leadership in religious research. She had been taught that people of other religions were wrong and without spirituality.

Then during a trip to India she met good and spiritual Hindus and the experience broadened her thinking. She wrote the book; *Encountering God: A Spiritual Journey from Bozeman to Banares*—Eck said "Through the years I have found my own faith not threatened but broadened and deepened by the study of Hindu, Buddhist, Muslim and Sikh traditions of faith...only as a Christian pluralist could I be faithful to the mystery and the presence of the one I call God. Being a Christian pluralist means daring to encounter people of different faith traditions and defining my faith not by its borders but by its roots."

Diana Eck may not know it but she is a member of the emerging religion of the global generation.

Isn't it the same face...the same mountain we are climbing, albeit by different paths? The Children of the new Global Order believe it is.

CHAPTER TWO

ॐ ✡ ☿ ☪ ✤ 🧘 🕉 ∞ ☯ ✝

BARBED WIRE AND AN AIRPLANE CRASH

When I was learning to fly an airplane, my instructor tried to teach me a valuable lesson. We were doing the pre-flight inspection and while doing an inspection to check wing and flap surfaces he asked me what the condition of the left wing was. I answered: "Well you were on that side of the airplane what did it look like to you?" He frowned and replied: "If you are going to stay alive as a pilot, never trust someone else's judgment. You are the captain, thus you must take responsibility. It is your life that is at stake when you are flying an airplane. If you rely on another, person remember the old Russian adage; 'Trust, but verify'."

As a young idealistic college student it was easy to trust other people. People who were older were even easier to trust. So I didn't really take the advice of my flying instructor seriously until one day a farmer in the Arkansas Ozarks asked me to fly up to his place and help him spot a lost cow. "You can land in my field" he said. So we went out and I walked the field, stepping it off to be sure it was level and long enough to land a Cherokee 140 single engine airplane. It was in a long valley with a wooded hill at one end and a farm road with an old widow's house surrounded by a stone wall at the other end. She had planted a large garden in front of her house and had put a fence around it to keep livestock out.

Crossing the mid section of the field was the remains of an old fence. There was just one old rusty strand of barbed wire left, drooping from fence post to fence post. The farmer said: "Don't worry about that, I'll take that old fence down before you come." I trusted him.

The next Sunday I was at the airport at sunrise. It was a beautiful cool crisp morning with calm winds perfect for flying. Two friends who had never flown in a private airplane asked if they could ride up with me. "Sure" I said, "It will be a new experience for you!"

As we approached the field, I had to descend steeply because the hill at one end was higher than I anticipated. With full flaps and power I set the plane wheels down in the grassy pasture and hit the brakes. But the grass was still wet with morning dew causing the wheels to slip on the uneven ground. The airplane was not slowing so I pressed down on the brakes harder while raising the flaps to put more weight on the wheels. Just at that instant I looked up ahead to see something that horrified me. It was not visible from the air but there in the pasture ahead still standing was that old fence with the strand of barbed wire waiting for us.

I put on full throttle and applied flaps but the grass seemed to claw at the wheels. The airplane was just below airspeed with the fence coming at us faster and faster. At the last moment I pulled up on the stick. The airplane lifted up, the front wheels just barely clearing the fence. But then I felt a sickening shudder. The rear tie down hook at the rear of the fuselage had hooked the strand

26

of barbed wire fence. While the airplane engine was roaring and clawing for altitude, the strand of wire was unwinding like a fishing line trying to drag the airplane down. The engine fought mightily but I could feel the barbed wire winning the battle as the airplane began to slow into a stall. The nose went up high then dropped and I could see the old widow's garden coming fast. We crashed through the garden fence burrowing and throwing dirt in every direction. The sound was deafening as we crashed through her rock wall tearing off both wings of the airplane. We came to a rough stop in a cloud of dust about 10 feet from her front porch just as she was walking out the door to go to church. She was stunned, watching as I turned off the ignition, fuel pump and gas valve and cried out to my passengers: "Get out quick, it might explode!" I didn't realize at that moment that there was no danger because the wings and gas tanks were somewhere behind the rock wall we had crashed through.

We fell out of the smoking plane to see the trail of destruction that we had left behind us. In that instant I realized that I had made a mistake by putting our lives in the hands of that farmer, who promised he would remove the fence. I was angry when I went to his farmhouse and asked him why he hadn't removed that fence. He just shrugged and said: "Oh, I just didn't get around to it."

I realized that he had a different agenda. You might say that he had a different set of values. His priorities were different than mine. His omission in removing that fence could have killed or maimed us. His lack of action had an enormous impact on our lives. Yet to him it was almost funny. He didn't seem to mind at all that we had crashed, destroyed property and been traumatized. For over a year after that event every time I heard a loud sound or our car hit a bump I relived that crash.

Some of the old institutional dogmas of the religious world are similar to that strand of old rusty barbed wire. Long past being of any use, they droop, hanging as an eyesore long past relevance. They can be dangerous just as that wire strand was when it hooked my airplane. The progressive and idealistic global generation sees the potential of a new world filled with love and intellect that is empowered by good will and peaceful intent. Responsible leaders will remove the old rusty barriers that can harm others or withhold progress. Irresponsible leaders will just "not get around to it" while they allow old tired dogmas to hang, blocking progress.

The global generation does not condemn any group. Indeed it accepts all religions. But it doesn't accept old rusty dogmas of judgmental attitudes or fanaticism. While the emerging religion can accept any institutional religion, its adherents will "trust but verify" to analyze if the dogmas have current relevance. The new world may require that bright minded people take the initiative to remove the old "fences" of outdated and archaic thought. That is not easy work. Dealing with the "barbs" of long established dogma and tradition can be painful. It is hard to remove and harder still to find responsible ways to dispose of the garbage of bad thinking. But if those who devised those "tired dogmas" won't (or can't) eliminate the problem it will be up to the global generation to clean up their mess.

Consider the problems the Catholic Church has had in the sexual abuse scandals. Like old rusty barbed wire, many regions of the church still have garbage hanging. Sometimes it is hidden by the undergrowth of time but it is still there, a hazard that can harm people.

Consider the problems of the conservative churches such as the Baptist denomination or the conservative Church of Christ, as they try to deal with the progressive elements of their denominations. The older smaller country churches hang on to older traditional dogmas while younger growing suburban churches tend to adopt more progressive concepts.

Consider the problems of Islam. The Shiites versus the Sunnis is a classic conflict of narrow tradition against positive intellectual growth. The radical fundamentalists of the Shiites are still preaching a dogma of Jihad from the 7th century, versus moderate Sunnis who want to merge and integrate Islam into the modern world.

Consider the Hindus with the divisions of the young college educated moderates who want peace and progress vs. the older sects who still cling to violence, war and hatred with roots back to the partition of India and Pakistan.

Consider the old traditional Jewish leaders who are still fighting battles of 30 years ago versus the younger moderates who are willing to give the Palestinians a homeland and live together in peace.

Consider the old hard line Communist leaders of China who still try to rule by repression and brute power. They dominate indigenous peoples such as the Tibetans with an iron hand with an old philosophy of sheer "might makes right". The more moderate Chinese businessmen and the great masses of the Buddhist population desire a more tolerant and enlightened approach of rule.

Consider the radical "anti-abortionists" in America who can justify bombing, vandalism and even killing in the name of Christianity versus educated people who don't condone violence.

Consider political leaders who still use the old "rusty" tools of manipulation through patriotism, or war to gain political power. They will war on weaker nations just to arouse patriotic fervor. They stand opposed to moderates and intellectuals who would call for peace and a positive fellowship of nations.

Consider powerful giant business interests that are motivated by greed and profits vs. responsible business leaders who are loyal to the interests of their employees, their communities and have initiated codes of ethics that give back to their communities. The conflict of philosophy is massive. The big boys have money and the power. But as corruption scandals arise and are exposed again and again, it is obvious that it is time for responsible leaders with values favoring "humanity" to come forth. They must temper corporate greed with social responsibility.

Consider the aberration of political systems where the very wealthy control politicians to the detriment of the vast majority of the people who have no wealth and desperately need honest and fair representation to help protect them. Politicians must again focus on helping the masses to live in peace and prosperity and stop favoring the rich.

Consider concentrations of wealth wherein 350 of the world's billionaires and 100 of the world's largest corporations control over 70% of the world's wealth. In the past 20 years more money has flowed into fewer hands than in all of history. This is even of greater concern when we consider that one third of the people of the world make less than $1 per day. While poverty grows at unprecedented rates those 300 billionaires make more money than over two billion people on earth combined! Then dream of the possibility of intellectual leaders creating tax policies and economic systems that might provide more opportunity and less suffering to those of the middle and lower classes.

The New York Times published a feature on July 14, 2002, about churches closing in the Midwestern part of the United States. The article focused on population declines in small town America and the many vacant churches left standing. The article missed a major point. The new global environment is impacting churches clearly in tangible ways. Higher and higher percentages of emerging people are moving away from institutional organized religion. They are not moving away from ethics or religious values, but they are moving away from the traditions, the politics, the control, the manipulation, and the limitations that traditional organized religion has come to represent.

We must teach, speak, and write to fill the vacuum left by the empty and unheard pulpits.

Unfortunately, there is also another trend among uneducated and poor classes. This level of society is also rejecting institutional religion and becoming more secular. But in this sector of society, the voice of the priest, preacher, or lama has been replaced by radio talk show hosts, fringe element radicals, or even sports or entertainment heroes. Thus in some levels of society, the poor and uneducated working people are becoming reactionaries with aggressive-compulsive emotional patterns, sometimes violent behavior tendencies. It is reminiscent of the growth of McCarthyism, Pol Pot, or Nazism.

Then there are more informed "educated" layers of society. They do not want to be called by any institutional name. They are global citizens, citizens of the world with a world view. There has never been a time when the need for the leadership and voices of enlightened people has been as great as it is now.

The trend in the Midwest is a glimpse of things coming. More and more vacant church buildings are coming available, in cities large and small. They are being converted to restaurants, commercial office buildings, schools, and day care centers.

The redefinition of religious loyalties is bound to change the landscape of America literally. Architects believe that the size of the building and the prominence of the buildings reflect the culture of that society. For example, in Mexico, when the Aztecs ruled, the pyramids represented the largest structure in the nation, and the most important social unifier of the culture. In Germany, during the period from 1600 AD to 1800 AD, the largest building in each community was a church with its steeple. In commercial and materialistic America of the 20th century, the banks and businesses have become the largest most prominent buildings of society, reflecting the capitalistic and emerging secular nature of this society.

What will the landscape and architecture influenced by the new global citizens of the 21st and 22nd century look like?

There will be prayer gardens, with sculptures, fountains and statues for reflection and meditation. There will be artistic monuments, stupas, and temples built. They will not be built for any one church or group but will be monuments to the blending and maturation of religious groups; they will preach acceptance, the commonality of love, and the one spirit of mankind. There will be a renewal of religious art, and thousands of this new generation will express themselves in creative and artistic pursuits. There will be centers of learning, study, and ethical research.

But institutions of church politics will be avoided because of the inherent nature of humans to build power structures around themselves and manipulate religious groups for control and power. There will be a vast population of people with no religious or ethical loyalties. They will require guidance. If the enlightened people of society don't provide this guidance, reactionaries of violence and hatred will, just as the Nazis took over civilized Germany in the 1930s.

In light of all of these examples, there is a thought that is easily lost. Revisit the story of my modern airplane and the old barbed wire fence that ended in disaster that Sunday morning back in 1969. We admit that an old rusty fence can destroy a modern airplane. Let me suggest a bright thought. What if some good responsible caring person had removed the old rusty fence? What if we had landed in that field and loaded up the farmer and found his lost cattle? What if we had enjoyed a perfect day of flying over the verdant Ozarks and done another human being a favor in the process? It could have been a perfect metaphor reflecting Louis Armstrong's song: "Oh what a wonderful world!" For the children of the global generation, the flowers facing the sun must live with the view of HOW THE WORLD CAN BE. That vision must be ever within us.

CHAPTER THREE

ॐ ✡ ☿ ☪ ✾ 🧘 ॐ ✝ ☯ ✝

BIRTH PAINS AND FUNDAMENTALISM

It is a struggle to face new ideas and to expand the mind. Even as a woman experiences birth pains, birthing new ideas can be painful. Some people fear new ideas and even education.

Dr. Sam Ghanty is a professor of economics in Cambodia. A great opportunity opened to him when a university in the USA gave him a scholarship to get his PhD. While in America his wife joined him, reluctantly leaving their children in Cambodia in the care of grandparents. One day Dr. Sam got a telegram from Cambodia. "Pol Pot has determined that since you are getting an education in America you are an enemy." His heart froze with concern for his children. When he and his wife returned to Cambodia, they learned in horror that their children, parents and entire family had been executed. Years later while floating on the Mei Kong River I asked him: "Dr. Sam, weren't you scared to stay in Cambodia after that?" Tears came to his eyes as he replied "We had already lost everything dear to us. All we could do now is come back and try to help our country recover." Dr. Ghanty came face to face with the fear of new ideas and education and dealt with it courageously.

It is obvious that those who benefit financially, feed on

and who are empowered by the traditional orders will fear or oppose the new emerging religion. But there is little that they will be able to do, for as the folk song of the sixties so aptly prophesied: "For the times they are a-changing…"

As people become more conversant with those of other faiths, their religious perspectives broaden. As they do business with and befriend people around the world with different traditions, as they interface with other cultures, they will find more things in common with people all over the world. It is hard to travel, to see and to observe people around the world without ultimately coming to the conclusion that we all are truly related. Yes we truly are brothers for we come from one source, one genetic ancestor. We have so much in common, far more than we have in opposition to one another.

Recently I received an e-mail from Deepak Nirula in India. He is a successful business executive who owns a hotel and other business ventures in his country. Our cultures, religions and backgrounds couldn't be more diverse. India is dominated by a Hindu culture. But in his letter he expressed love and respect and appreciation for an article I published on Global Trends. This man, so different, so far away, has bonded and become a "brother" to me intellectually. We share stories and jokes and concerns and thoughts about our world. We are "one" and he illustrates the type of relationship I'm describing. It would be our hope and dream for the realization of a universal brotherhood of man, and it would seem to be within reach.

I remember as a young man, being a member of a small sect called the "Church of Christ." When I traveled from

Texas, through Arkansas, Missouri, and Tennessee, I could always count on having friends if I stopped at a Church of Christ. This group was tight knit and would always treat a "brother" with hospitality and generosity. As long as I could find a Church of Christ, no matter how far I was from home and how broke I was, I knew that the "brethren" would always offer me a meal, and if I needed it, a place to stay. That is the kind of brotherhood I can see for the "new brotherhood of the global generation ."

The people who are a part of this "movement" are not necessarily young. R.C. Leonard was a bomber pilot for the U.S. air force stationed in Asia during World War Two. While in Asia he often flew over the Himalayas. He once said, "I was flying with my co-pilot and good friend one day when we ran into anti-aircraft flack. I looked over, and his head had been blown off. When that happens, it makes you think more about prayer and religion." He began studying great religious thinkers. Forty years later, when I was a bank president, R.C. was one of my Vice Presidents. I was intrigued that every day he wrote a prayer or inspirational verse and put it on my desk. That happened every day for **two** years, and finally I asked him about his intellectual quest. "I don't go out and try to evangelize or convert people to a religion" he said, "but I have studied all of the great religions. There is a universal brotherhood. Each of us has good within us and with encouragement and spiritual grooming, each person can blossom." I realized that this man had lived a long, productive life, filled with spiritual study and insight. There were deeper levels of his intellect than showed on the surface. In his late seventies he was a member of the "new global generation". R.C. is a man of depth - devoting specific energies to encourage and stimulate others. When

I was a bank president, he would occasionally walk into my office and say: "I see the God in you." It was years later that I realized he was actually paraphrasing "Namaste," the greeting of respect of India.

The University Christian Church of Fort Worth, Texas is next to the campus of Texas Christian University. This old, established congregation invited me to teach a series of comparative parallels of Buddhist teaching and Christian teaching. I taught a course that lasted for several weeks. In our study, the class discovered over forty teachings of Christ, including some parables that were also taught by Buddha. BUT Buddha lived and died some 500 years BEFORE Christ was born! Rather than seeing this as a threat to our traditional beliefs, the class embraced this as enrichment and a broadening factor to our faith and knowledge.

This is a perfect example of how broader enlightenment and acceptance of multi-cultural thinking is taking place, and how it can enrich us, even if we still work and worship within the confines of a traditional institutional organization. Those institutions that recognize and accept this vast sociological change may embrace it and grow. Those which do not will experience attrition. Acceptance of multi-cultural thinking is a part of the mental process of the new "global citizen." It is a joyful and exciting journey that provides new vistas at every turn!

THE PROBLEM OF FUNDAMENTALISM

But in light of the above, fundamentalists of all religions will have the most difficult time with the new birth of religious thought.

Sectarian Fundamentalism has come to be understood as a thought system that suggests that only the most basic and fundamental views of a religion are important. In the Christian world, fundamentalists might ignore 2000 years of scholarship and go back to "the Bible only" for direction. Indeed some might accept only "ancient" original languages as authoritarian sources. In Islam, they might return to the life of Mohammed and only look at his life for direction. The unfortunate part of this is that fundamentalists tend to see black and white, while life forces us to see that there are gray areas requiring grace, love and judgment. Perhaps that is why Buddha put aside extremism on either end of the religious spectrum and suggested that people take the "middle way"…the way of moderation in life and religion.

Charles Kimball in his book: *When Religion Becomes Evil* cites five warning signs of corruption in religion. They are:

1. Absolute Truth Claims

2. Blind Obedience

3. Establishing the "Ideal" Time

4. The End Justifies Any Means

5. Declaring Holy War

I recommend his book, because he comes from a background of being a Baptist Minister and is also a man who has studied world religions. His perspective is broad and excellent. I have identified a similar but longer list of characteristics of Fundamentalism that can be dangerous. Some of the common alarming characteristics are:

1. **EXCLUSIVISM:** Fundamentalists tend to believe they are the only ones who have "THE" truth.

2. **JUDGEMENTALISM:** Fundamentalists tend to judge anyone not in their sect as "damned" "going to hell" "inferior" or "infidels".

3. **RADICAL ACTIVISM:** Fundamentalists tend to be willing to take strong actions in defense of their belief, sometimes violent. Some would die for their beliefs. Some exhibit aggressive compulsive behavior and would do harm or even try to destroy opponents.

4. **RULE OF LAW VERSUS RULE FAVORING PEOPLE:** Fundamentalists generally create strict systems and rules and they will enforce these rules even if it hurts people. The "law" takes precedence over humanity.

5. **INTIMIDATION:** Fundamentalists often use intimidation or force to achieve their goals.

6. **VIOLENCE:** Sometimes fundamentalist systems in love of "law" above love of people find it acceptable to destroy people to achieve their goals.

7. **TYRANNY OF THE WEAKER BROTHER:** Fundamentalists often put themselves in the position of being the weaker brother, the downtrodden, or the one who is persecuted. They then use a position of the "tyranny of the weaker brother" to dominate

others. Spinning this perspective to persecute or manipulate others to do their will.

8. One danger of fundamentalism is its **RADICAL ENERGY**. A fundamentalist can ultimately justify the destruction of other people, tearing apart of relationships or even killing and war to achieve his "**defense of truth**". That is a characteristic that is rampant in much of the religious world.

Fundamentalism in Islam, Hinduism, Judaism, Communism and Christianity have been the source of enormous violence, killing, political instability and harm to people. Furthermore, fundamental extremism appears to be growing.

The only way to combat fundamentalism is through love, education and free thought. Even this is often not successful. Fundamentalism has no place in the religion of the new enlightened global generation. But often, the mindset of enlightened people is such that they are not willing to undergo violence, nor do they zest the battle for truth. Often, enlightened people simply back away from fundamentalists, (thinking everyone has a right to his belief) and let them take control of institutions and organizations. Thus situations emerge where fundamentalists gradually take over schools, clubs, boards, cities, churches, and even governments. Then, the fundamentalists change the system to see to it that there is no "freedom of belief". Thus, the moderates and enlightened people find themselves outlawed. Enlightened people must meet fundamentalism with intelligence, firmness, and a willingness to teach with love, but also not to yield to the intimidation of emotionally driven radicals. Fundamentalists fear, above all, the open exchange of ideas, free speech, uncensored communication and open interaction. They will try to sensor, close down, control and monitor to achieve limitation of intellectual freedom. When you observe the specter of control and censorship, it is time to put up a red flag to see if there is a hidden agenda that might ultimately destroy freedom of thought.

Some of the people to be concerned about are those with a cultural superiority complex.

CULTURAL SUPERIORITY COMPLEX

Why do humans tend to believe that our group, our city, our religion, school, nation, culture, or lifestyle is the superior one? There is an old slave saying: "There is only one perfect person in the world, AND YOU AREN'T HIM." If we all applied that thought the world would be a better place.

Linda Colley is a historian at the London School of Economics. In her book *Britons: Forging the Nation, 1707-1837* she points out that nationalism was contrived and that leaders used religion to consolidate their own power, turning themselves into both political and religious leaders. Religious passion was the one popular emotion that could bring the masses into the streets, and Europe's rulers considered it the most powerful of forces. Therefore it was considered politically smart to try to teach religious and political groups that 'they were the superior ones'.

Anthony Marx of Columbia University points out the relationship of religious intolerance and political power and how King Ferdinand and Queen Isabella helped form the Kingdom of Spain by use of religious fervor and "exclusionary nationalism." He said it was crucial for politicians and religious leaders to define a community as "us and them." His book Faith *in Nation: Exclusionary Origins of Nationalism* is worth reviewing.

However, this was nothing new. Ancient American Indians called themselves "THE people." Some African tribes call their location "THE center of the universe." Hindu peoples mark places such as Banares (Varanasi) as "THE Holy center," even as Jewish people mark Jerusalem as the "City of GOD". The ancient Jews called themselves "God's People", as do modern Christians. The implications are that if you aren't in *their* group you are somehow diminished or inferior. You could even be an infidel or doomed to eternal damnation. Some political nationalists use the same psychology to create political "exclusionary" nationalism, especially if the politicians want to start a war or strengthen a political position. Hitler and his Nazi's were brilliant in the use of this technique.

Mongolians considered Karakarum (Chinghis Khan's capital) to be the center of the world. This type of thinking applies to religions. In the backwoods of Arkansas or the small towns of West Texas, the tiny little villages have a Church of Christ, Baptist Church, Methodist Church and a Catholic Church. I was raised in a small church that taught that if you were not a member of **that** particular church, you were doomed to eternal hell fire when you died. Thus there was a strange paradox of living, working and having friendships with all of our neighbors. We liked them but thought that they were all heretics and doomed to Hell because they were not of our sect.

Fortunately, sects such as it have matured with education and affluence, and men like Bob Collier (a west Texas pharmacist and businessman) have come into leadership positions. Bob, like many west Texans before him, understands human compassion and kindness and does not engage in destruction of people by the use of religious doctrine. Ask any person in Post, Texas, and they can tell story after story of his generosity of spirit. Bob led the way in ecumenical thought by starting a sunrise meeting where all spiritual leaders were invited, regardless of their denominational affiliation. Generations of people have benefited by his leadership.

Bob recognized early in his life that attitudes of exclusionary judgementalism can be found everywhere. Recently an American reporter at a school in Pakistan sat with young students and was surprised when they told him that although they liked him personally, someday they would kill him because he was an infidel. Indeed in an article in the *New York Times* (5/31/03), Alexander Stille pointed out that the philosophical prevalence of the volatile mixture of intolerance, religious fanaticism and political nationalism as a theory is growing.

After 9/11, there were thousands of incidents of people killing, beating, or burning the premises of Islamic people in the United States. Often, the people were not even Islamic. But ignorant Americans targeted people with oriental or Asian dress anyway, thinking that if they spoke with a strange accent, they must be the bad guys. Hindus, Sieks, even people from Israel, were mistaken for Muslims and persecuted. This was ironic because just two years earlier when radical fundamentalist Hindus burned an Australian Christian missionary to death in his car, over one hundred thousand Muslims demonstrated in Delhi, India supporting "tolerance and the right of religious freedom."

Why do we judge others (people outside OUR group) as wrong or inferior? Worse, why do we judge them as evil or evil-doers?

Why does each culture think that it is the center of the universe?

Their thinking evolves from insecurity and the ego, the "I," or the loneliness of existence. We are trapped in a body of flesh (or at least we perceive that we are). We believe that we are the center because that is our most primitive and fundamental instinct. Thus, when we make a friend with common beliefs, he shares our "ego" and takes a bit of the loneliness, fear and despair away. He helps us to imagine that we aren't so finite.

Expand it to a group, a political party, a city, a province, a state, a nation, club, corporation, army or religion, and the "I" expands to the "us" or the "superior WE" as the center.

What if we approach existence differently? What if we accept a premise that we aren't trapped in a body? What if we stretch to believe that our spirit, our ideas, our energy is a part of a much larger whole? Consider that whole, that interaction and expansion of our energy blending with the energy of the world as a means of teaching us that we are all a part of each other in this more realistic dimension of reality.

In this dimension, suddenly we realize something. We

45

are not alone. We are not inferior. We are not trapped. We don't have to judge others, destroy others, war on others. We, rather, as a part of other nations, religions, groups, see that we have so much more compassion and interaction because we are a part of them, and they are a part of us. We can better try to understand the superficial differences and then see the real things that we have in common.

Yes, on one level, we may dress differently, eat different foods, enjoy different music, and have a different history, language, and religion. But on a deeper level, we find that we share concepts of love, the ethic of helping one another, and the sense of compassion for those who need it. We share the concepts of caring for family, the dignity of work and achievement, the joy of loved ones, the aspiration to find some meaning in life...thus to feel loved and respected.

As we understand the common fears of mankind, the common despair of the random nature of life, we then begin to eliminate fear and despair because we identify with our fellow wanderers. In reality we are multicultural, whether we want to be or not. We can put up artificial walls, rules, and restrictions, but we cannot avoid the fact that we are one with the world: humanity is our brother. When we war on the world, we war on ourselves. If we attack another, we are attacking ourselves. If we are filled with jealousy, hatred, or anger, we are eating away at ourselves.

In preparation for the war on Iraq, a news reporter showed a video clip from Baghdad. On the streets, in the markets, were old grandmothers shopping and buying food for their families. There were children with shining faces, smiling and playing. As I saw these elderly women and these young innocent children, I could not bear the thought that an American bomb could fall on them and blow them into oblivion.

It was then that I realized both the power and the responsibility of being Multi-Cultural. Multi-Cultural thinking implies that we are humanists, that we love and care for humanity. To put it more specifically, we have compassion for human beings. We care. It is an awesome thought. But one that carries with it the responsibility to energize and use our minds and wills to stop injustice and war at every opportunity. We cannot sit idly and watch.

THE IRONY OF MULTICULTURALISM

Once we have adopted a global perspective we cannot turn back. It will impact every aspect of our thinking. Ken Wilber, in his book: A BRIEF HISTORY OF EVERYTHING describes a conflict that multicultural thinkers must deal with. If multiculturalists take a position that religion is equal or that everyone is equal, then no ethical or moral stand is better than any other! Thus the conflict emerges as some multiculturalists exhibit vicious intolerance for intolerance, all in the name of tolerance. Like the hippie who said: "I hate people who hate!"

The global generation must realize that there is a danger of becoming "a bunch of elitists trying to outlaw everybody else's elitisms." (Wilber)

Look at Hitler's Nazis or McCarthy's congressional investigations, or the Taliban's religious police. Groups like this cannot compare with the precepts of Jesus or Buddha. Therefore what do we do? Should we judge? How do we keep from becoming what we hate? How do we avoid fragmenting and retribalization of the world?

The answer is to maintain an attitude of tolerance and curiosity that seeks truth. This requires a willingness to analyze the depth of thought systems to determine the fruits of that system.

Disciples of Jesus dealt with this in the Bible. There were a variety of teachings and teachers and the question of who to follow came up. "How do we know which teachings are right?" came the question.

"By their fruits you shall know them." was the reply.

The ultimate test of truth, goodness and merit of a philosophy is its level of compassion and how it impacts the lives of people.

If a philosophy hurts people, if it does not show compassion, if it is not driven by and does not result in love then something is wrong. If it does not elevate humanity then the philosophy is to be ignored or avoided. But when a thought system helps people, results in compassion and love, then there is a religion to study! If it elevates humanity and feeds the spirit, THAT is a philosophy to mine for its treasures.

CHAPTER FOUR

THE NATURE OF GOD

One of the questions that this generation continues to ask is: "In the face of pain, and suffering, what is the nature of God, or Shiva or Allah?" The question is related to the question of Why? Especially in tragedy, such as 9/11, we must ask, would a loving and omnipotent God allow so much pain and suffering in those he loved? Can we broaden our understanding of the concept of God? Consider the following to start you on your intellectual journey to better understand the nature of God.

It is risky to try to describe God. You tell me that you are in love with a beautiful woman, but when I ask you 'What is the color of her hair, what is the color of her eyes, what is her name?' If you don't know, I don't believe you are really in love with something real. Your notion of God may be vague like that, not having to do with reality. It is difficult to define God by old Theological theories. There may be a better way. Let us see what scholars say about God.

There are several views of God. Here are a few:

1. **ABSOLUTELY SOVEREIGN OMNIPOTENT God.**
   Exemplified by the statement; "My God is in control of all things" You might pose the question: If a man loved his child, would he let it walk into a giant shredding machine and be shredded to pieces?" No

loving father would do that. Would a loving God? A quick response might be, "Well, God let his son suffer and die on the cross." But, think of it.

Does your God actually control **every event** in life? This is hard for most people to allow.

2. **SOVEREIGN OMNIPOTENT GOD THAT "ALLOWS SUFFERING".** To deal with the above conflicts, many in the world have come to believe in a God who is omnipotent and sovereign, but, they give God some relief from responsibility by moving the responsibility to humanity with the logic of choice. The argument generally goes like this. God doesn't cause bad things to happen, because he gives us a choice. Therefore all of the evil and painful events are our fault because of bad choices. An example of this is when the evangelist Jerry Falwell said that 9/11 was our fault because the United States allows abortions and homosexuals in the USA. Back to the original thesis, this God is still in control, he just moves back a little sometimes. Like the loving father, who lets his child "make the choice" to walk into a giant shredding machine. This view of God still implies that he is in charge, still has the power, but he is willing to allow horror, pain and suffering, because **we** made the wrong choices. Think about it. This is a difficult idea to accept.

Would a loving father allow terrible pain, and suffering upon his children?

3. The ancients, starting with the Greeks, and then developed further by Augustine, came up with a line of thought, that was later further developed into yet

a different concept by Calvinists. It was **the CLOCKMAKER GOD**. In this scenario, God created the universe and all in it to function like a clock. He is no longer directly involved with daily operations...all is set to work as it works. God has set it in motion, and now sits back and watches. Thus, this God has no daily interaction with our lives, nor does he change events. When the clock stops, then there will be an accounting, all pre-ordained by the precise movements of the "clock" of the universe. Several hundred years later, those who believed in pre-destination took it one step further, and said that God predestined the lives of every human on earth, and that humans had no choice as to the ultimate conclusion of things.

The clockmaker makes it easier to accept that which is hard to understand about suffering and pain, for this God is aloof and distant.

4. **GENERAL GOD.** This concept considers God in an overwhelming spiritual war, and thus he is engaged in battles with evil. In these constant battles, God is willing to allow the death and suffering of a few here and there, to win the overall war. Some are "dispensable" for the greater good. He may lose a battle, but ultimately will win the war. He is like the general of the U.S.A. who when an American missile drifted and killed 30 or 40 women and children in a public market said: "Regrettable but these things happen in war".

God as a "General" satisfies the needs of some people to accept the calamity and pain of life. But this God isn't very helpful to the victims of pain and suffering.

5. **BEGGAR GOD.** This idea is that God is filled with love, and grief at our sinfulness, and he stands outside the door, begging for us to come to him. He loves us very much, but will not get personally involved with our lives until and unless we open the door, and respond to His pleas for us to come to Him, love Him, worship and accept Him.

This God is sometimes portrayed as a God who needs humanity and cries in heavenly tears when we don't love him.

6. **"I AM" GOD.** Many psychologists believe that the ultimate basic concept of God for each individual is that our concept of God ultimately defines who we are.

Indeed the idea is that our mind, our brain, our spirit, all need to believe in a God, but that identity is ultimately our deepest self. God is our deepest psyche. God is our identity, our ego, our self perception. I AM is the basic cry of all humanity, crying for the meaning of existence.

7. **PANTHEISTS, ANIMISTS.** Pantheists believe that God is evident in the trees, rocks, all of nature. This belief is prevalent in cultures with roots in nature. The most primitives sometime worship the actual symbols, the trees, rocks, mountains, sun, moon or stars. Animists tend to worship animals, snakes, fish or birds. The more advanced believe that these are only physical manifestations symbolizing the "great spirit".

Do you feel close to God when you are in nature?

8. **ANTHROPOMORPHS!** Then, there is the approach that says that all of the above views of God have some truth, but that we are thinking in the wrong perspective. This is the concept of the ANTHROPOMORPHED God. Various writers of Hebrew and Christian literature have "anthropomorphed" the concept of God. This concept suggests that we have made God "human like" so that we can understand Him thus we anthropomorphize Him. Humans give him human traits (like we do a dog, a car or even a computer). We name Him, we try to make Him like us, and we try to understand Him from our perspective. The Ancient Christian Theologian, Thomasius called God, "the absolute personality".

This approach tends to put God in a box, to make Him small enough for us to understand, but does not do justice to the awesome nature of a God that creates not only us, but our world, our universe. But, it historically has been used, both in and out of the scriptures, as a necessity, especially to help the most basic believers to have a faith, and a prayer life to a "God" that they can understand.

Thus millions create images or statues to better help them visualize a "man-like" God. Some might think of God as being white, male, with a long white beard like Charlton Hesston's portrayal of Moses. Some want to think of him like a personal grandfather. One of the problems with this is that God evidently sent his son, in an expressed purpose to bridge the gap between his vastness, and the needs of man. Jesus was sent as the "Human" or anthropomorphic emissary for God...for the God that we see in the

Bible was simply so awesome. One example is when Moses came back from the mountain in a different aura or when Paul was blinded by the light of God on the road to Damascus. The inconsistency comes when we review other scriptures that speak of God in terms so vast and un-humanlike as "not to be conceived or imagined by man".

OTHER CONCEPTS OF GOD: There are many diverse concepts illustrated by a woman who walked into our import shop and said: "Church members carrying a big floppy Bible came to my home one night and announced that they were there to break me away from the Unity Church. They wanted to tell me about their concept of God. I told them that in my opinion, that SHE was filled with love, grace and power. SHE didn't have to go walking door to door with a floppy Bible to intimidate people into believing in her. They said they were going to stay in my house until I came around. I closed the door of my bedroom and went to bed. The next morning, they were gone. Their concept of God was much different than mine."

MORE CONCEPTS OF GOD

- Plato: God is pure being."

- Paul: Romans 16:26 "eternal God"

- II Cor 3:27 "Lord is Spirit"

- Ancient Christian Theologian, Melanchthon "God is a spiritual essence"

- Professor W. Adams Brown said: "God is an unseen being"

- Professor Herbert Spencer : "God is an inscrutable power manifested to us through all phenomena"

- Biblical statements:

God is love

God is light

God is the way

God is the Trust

God is Almighty

God is the Rock

God is Holy

"No house or place can contain Him"

God inhabits eternity

God is Eternal

God's thoughts and ways transcend those of men

God is the first and the last

God is like a consuming fire

God is like "fire...brilliant light...like the appearance of a rainbow...radiance"

"the appearance of the likeness of the glory of the Lord"

Exodus 3:2-4, 19-18, 24:17 Different forms of god, "fire, smoke and clouds"

"I AM" YAHWEH

Hebrew: ha yah "to be"

"I AM THAT I AM"

God brought earth stars and rivers to battle... Judges 5:4, 20, 21

Sun and moon stands still... Joshua 10:12-13

Joseph Campbell, the great religious philosopher said: "My God has a thousand faces, all leading to an understanding of God". He suggested that reading about God in a book is like reading a menu in a restaurant. We don't eat the menu. It simply gives us some idea of what the meal to come might be like. The menu describes what we have the ability to enjoy and participate in. Some people stop at the menu...some worship the menu, the description, code book, or symbols. He says, "Don't confuse the description of God, the Bible, the Torah, or the "physical or written description" of Shiva, or Buddha, or Allah, or Yahweh, or the Great Spirit, with God...that is simply the menu, a window that leads to understand the feast to come". His line of thought suggests that God is so vast, so powerful, such an energy in us, above us, before us, behind us, a concept of pure energy. He is so vast that to understand him would be to try to go to the beach and put the ocean into a coke bottle. The bottle would dematerialize. So our brains, because we cannot comprehend the "fullness of God would simply not be able to fully take in or understand this concept we call God".

Robert Schuler, after 9/11 said; "We can see God, in the reaction of heroism and love by those who responded to the tragedy. There, in those firemen, you can see the face of God". Others have said that God is when you are "Singing your song", when you are inspired by some event of love or beauty.

Handel said that he saw the face of God as he was composing the Messiah during the Hallelujah chorus. To him the inspiration of music was a connection with the divine energy.

The 12th Century text **BOOK OF THE TWENTY FOUR PHILOSOPHERS** says: "God is an intelligible sphere" (intelligible means known to the mind) "an intelligible sphere whose center is everywhere and circumference nowhere".

Swami Vivekenanda, a Hindu, spoke in 1893 in Chicago and said: "At the very outset I may tell you there is no polytheism in India. Hindu Gods represent different aspects of a single divine reality. The ancient Veda says 'In and through every particle of matter and force stands ONE, through whose command the wind blows, the fire burns, the clouds rain, and death stalks upon the earth."

Mukunda was popular as a holy man, born in India in 1893, and was said to have remarkable insights. He said: "there is a state called cosmic consciousness. My sense of identity was no longer narrowly confined to a body but embraced the circumambient atoms. People on distant streets seemed to be moving gently over my own remote periphery". He associated Albert Einstein's pursuit of a unified field theory which the great physicists hoped would account for every force from electricity to gravity with a single underlying cause, with the Hindu belief that beneath the apparent diversity of the universe lays a single reality.

Buddhists predated Christianity with the foundation belief and principal that life is suffering. They begin with that basic premise first. But, through compassion, meditation, inner peace, love and service to others, humans can find "nirvana" or a state of bliss and enlightenment. One of the most important aspects of Buddhist thought is that each human must take full responsibility for his thoughts and his actions, and not blame it on some external idea, influence or God. Through compassion, meditation, and self discipline, Buddhist's believe that humanity can touch or become part of a powerful energy of purity. They call it "enlightenment" or "Nirvana".

Could it be that all religions are simply man's simple way of trying to connect, to understand the vastness of God? That all of these religious symbols, stories, images, are simply windows or doorways to peeking in and touching a bit of the all powerful energy we call God? In many ways we belittle God, we make him smaller, we attempt to put our barriers on him, by our feeble "definitions" of God. He is all of the definitions, all of the characteristics, in them and of them all. And God is none of them as well. He is bigger and vaster than any definition. He is all power, all good, all energy, all logic, beauty, order, and love. God can even take the form of what **we** perceive to be pain, suffering, or even tragic events.

Could it be that this energy we call God, is so pervasive, so profound that it permeates every aspect of our existence? But, that we become so distracted with the daily events of our lives, that our mind, our eyes, our hearts, don't often feel or sense the power available to us?

If we think of God as pure, positive light, pure positive energy, pure love, pure balance, pure logic, pure power, pure goodness, then, the problem of suffering, the problem of pain becomes irrelevant. This energy does not have to have human characteristics. Suffering is as basic to life, as life. In dealing with suffering with compassion, with love, kindness, logic, order, peace, beauty, we then begin to touch the face of God and unleash this energy within us.

DEFINITION OF GOD? Can you define a power that is beyond all human language and measurement?

There is no way that we, as simple humans can define God, without putting constraints on what God is...his vastness...

"God cannot be experienced through notions and concepts...St. John Chrysosostom wrote: 'Let us invoke Him as the inexpressible God, incomprehensible, invisible, and unknowable. Let us avow that He surpasses all power of human speech, that He eludes the grasp of every mortal intelligence, that the angels cannot penetrate Him, nor the seraphim see Him in full clarity, nor the cherubim fully understand Him. For He is invisible to the principalities and powers, the virtues of all creatures without exception, only the Son and Holy Spirit know Him.'...the Son and the Holy Spirit have direct access to God because they are free from ideas and images of God." ...Thich Nhat Hanh, Vietnamese Scholar on Buddhism and Christianity

Saint Gregory of Nyssa, of the Eastern Orthodox Church, wrote: "Night designates the contemplation of invisible things after the manner of Moses, who entered into the darkness where God was, this God who makes of darkness His hiding place. Surrounded by the living night the soul seeks Him who is hidden in darkness. She (the soul) possesses indeed the love of Him who she seeks, but the beloved escapes the grasp of her thoughts."

Therefore…God must be the object of daily experience. People who rely solely on primitive images, tools, statues, paintings, Bibles, tapes, books, theologies, one day will no longer sustain their joy, peace, and happiness. God must be experienced to be known. While an image may serve as a useful tool, it cannot take the place of the spiritual experience of God.

After reviewing all of these concepts of god, we can make 3 definitive comments that are very similar, but have subtle differences:

1. *We can **add definition** to our understanding of this energy, this **God**, by the way we respond to the suffering around us.*

   This only adds color to our basic understanding of God…a full understanding of God is beyond humanity BUT if we feel anger, hatred, pain, sorrow, jealousy, stress or negative emotions then compassion in the light of suffering is a path to understanding, "feeling", knowing God in our hearts.

2. *We **define our faith**, and the genuineness and the depth of our faith by the way we respond to the suffering around us.*

3. **Ironically, we define ourselves**, by the way we respond to the events of life, pain, sorrow, loss, stress and suffering…

In summary, I offer this metaphor, to help understand the nature of God

We as individuals are like waves of the ocean. You are a wave. You look around, and there are thousands of you. Sometimes you are a big wave, full of energy, and sometimes you are a little wave. Sometimes you might just be a swell in the ocean. But when you finally are gone, have you disappeared? Only in one dimension. For, although you may cease to be a wave, you are still water.

That is how it is with us and with God. We may die, but we still continue to be spiritual beings, "water". And under the water there is vast depth, it doesn't even matter what is going on at the surface, - storms or calm -, for underneath there is such vastness you realize that you and all of the waves are of one energy. As individuals, we live for a while with what appears to be separate identities... we are all part of one another, and part of something far more lasting. So it is with God. He may have a thousand faces, all of which seem specific or individualistic, but God is of all things, and all things are a part of Him, in a different dimension. A dimension so vast, so deep, so wide, that we cannot encompass it, we cannot take it in. But, it is beautiful...an energy so vast, that only an eternity will give time to fully explore it. We are waves for a while...but before we were a wave, while we are a wave and after we cease to be a wave...we are always water. We are human beings for a while, but before, during and after our lives, we are something deeper... spiritual beings. God may come and manifest Himself as fire, flood, angels, a savior, an enlightened one, lightening, or show a thousand faces...but ultimately God is a vast spiritual ocean...of which we are from, of, and a part of, and in which we will eventually merge. That merging may be called "heaven" by Christians and Jews. It may be "Nirvana" for Buddhists. Whatever it is called, it is the ultimate merging with pure joy, love, energy, truth, power, light, and enlightenment.

CHAPTER FIVE

ॐ ✡ ♆ ☪ ❈ 🧘 ॐ ∞ ☯ ✝

CALL FROM TIBET

Tibet called. For years Tibet called and got a "busy" signal. But finally Tibet got through and gave me no choice. My wife said; "Who was that?" My only answer was: "Tibet called, and said that I must come. It is time." And so I went. Tibet opened spiritual dimensions and provided perspective. Tibet helped me to write this book. For as she told the story of the systematic destruction of institutional religion, she also demonstrated the power of internal faith. Tibet taught me the lasting power of religious energy that cannot be destroyed or fully or solely contained in temples.

It is a rare circumstance when one gets the opportunity to see something unique first hand. Tibet has many unique things to offer. Home of the highest mountains on earth, it is called The "Roof of the World". Some of the most significant geography on the planet rises from Tibet. But the most unique thing about Tibet is its religious heritage. Tibetans are probably the most religious people on earth. They are true believes devoted to their faith. They still believe in magic. Perhaps because of that faith, magical things are still there for them. Those colorful temples hidden away at altitudes unrealized in most nations provide a history and a mystique that is unparalleled anywhere on earth. The caves at the cliffs of Drak Yerpa have been a breeding ground for thinkers, seekers, searchers and visionaries for 2,000 years. Even in this modern age they are still destinations for seekers from throughout the world hoping to find something that institutional religion has lost or has not given them.

Modern Tibet is an oxymoron. The Chinese have built a few blocks of modern streets and buildings in Lhasa, but walk four blocks away from this modern façade section and old Tibet still exists. The old buildings slightly sloping inward for structural strength have colorful design and woodwork testifying to the endurance of the Tibetan culture. It is a land of marvelous contrast where the most secular, atheistic, anti-traditional culture on earth, Communist China, came to head on confrontation with the most religious and perhaps most devout culture on earth. China won every military battle, but was unable to destroy the culture and make it submit to Chinese norms. China also pursued complex and broad ranging social engineering to change Buddhist Tibet into Communist China. The Chinese called their invasion the *Liberation* of Tibet. It is telling that when a powerful nation wants to bully their way into a country and force their ways on a culture, they call it liberation. I recall a cartoon in the United States during the second war on Iraq. It depicted an American child watching the T.V. reports of U.S. bombing in Baghdad. The child looked up at his mother and said: "I hope that they don't decide to liberate me!" Surely the Tibetan people felt the same way about China.

Look at the results of the Chinese liberation of Tibet. China banned teaching the Tibetan language in schools, because they said it was a religious language. And yet after 50 years of domination the people still speak Tibetan. China destroyed over 8,000 temples and monasteries as well as thousands of stupas and holy shrines. They pillaged and hauled off statues, art and precious historical icons. But Tibetans have rebuilt many of the temples and slowly are replacing the lost art with new pieces. Time after time I witnessed penniless Tibetans rebuilding their temples brick by brick, mixing straw with mud to make their brick. The Chinese frowned on public display of religion. But on any morning in Lhasa at sunrise there is an example, almost a miracle of religious freedom in a place where the conqueror practices suppression of religion. As if by magic religious believers appear by the hundreds, perhaps thousands. Quietly walking with prayer wheels or mala's (rosaries) in hand, Tibetans walk toward the Potala. The Potala was the home of the Dalai Lama their spiritual and political leader before China "liberated" them. There the Tibetans walk praying quietly in a circle that is at least 2 miles in diameter around the Potala. They are praying and spinning prayer wheels with every step. Quietly they attest to their victory over the Chinese communist efforts to destroy their religion and their faith. These people are unique in the world in that they have been persecuted, their temples destroyed, their farms and property taken away from them, and some have seen their monks, even family members killed or imprisoned because of their faith. But they still walk with prayer wheels and malas in hand quietly praying their traditional mantra: "Ohm mani padne hen" ("All hail to the lotus in the jewel") Or loosely interpreted; "We praise and worship the concept of 'enlightenment' that is derived from the Jewel (the object of great value and wealth) that can be seen through the Dharma, the Sangha, and the Buddha. The Dharma is the body of teachings. The Sangha is the fellowship of fellow believers. The Buddha is the one who found enlightenment and gave the example of how others could follow suit. Tibetans

65

believe that we all inherently have the Buddha nature within.

This is what the Tibetans have that is so unique in the world. It is an institutional faith, a group, a teaching and a religion that still lives and is still worth living and dying for. It is a religion that still has the magic of faith, prayer, commitment and reverence. It is a religion that is enduring. Tibet has a religion that seems to be growing even in the secular West. It seems to be growing, albeit quietly and underground even in China where affluent businessmen quietly invest in Buddhist temples and contribute to orphanages, hospitals, and new monuments.

But Tibetan religion is not the reality for most people of the global generation. In fact, neither is Christianity, Judaism, Islam, Hinduism, Krishna or any of the major institutional religions. This new generation consists of educated people young and old who are familiar with communications and computer technology. They enjoy a world made smaller by fast inexpensive and available travel enabling them to interact with other cultures. They enjoy communication with peoples that 50 years ago were so far removed that the distance, expense and delays of communication were prohibitive. Today this generation's playground is the entire world. They speak, joke, and exchange ideas with people far removed by distance but close by technology. Who would have dreamed that a man in his Manhattan, New York apartment could at the press of a few buttons speak to, send photos or documents to a tribal chief in Africa, a Buddhist monk in a cave in the Himalayas, or a factory silk worker in India, at the speed of light? And the cost, thanks to the Internet, is almost free.

With these technologies, borders are no longer the barriers they once were. Religious prohibitions against communicating with those different than us are no longer effective. Political and legal barriers to the free exchange of ideas cannot stop the Internet, the fax, the television, and the telephone.

Is it no wonder that this global generation is better informed, more understanding and more tolerant than prior generations have been?

It is thus appropriate to document the emerging religion of the new global generation. It has powerful implications. Throughout history, powerful nations and leaders have used religion to accomplish their political, economic, social or military goals. Often, as in the case of China's *liberation* of Tibet, powerful nations try to destroy or repress institutional religion. The reason is because institutional religion can be a threat to the control and power of political regimes. But the religion of the new global generation is not institutionalized. Does this make it non-threatening and of no power? On the contrary, the very absence of buildings, headquarters, temples and an organized system may make this new religion more powerful because it can quietly morph events without political and emotional rhetoric that often is associated with religious movements. It simply becomes integrated into the mentality, the culture or ethical norms of society. That is happening at an accelerating pace worldwide.

TIBETAN HERMITS

I learned something interesting about sacred places on a mountain in Tibet called Drak Yerpa. Here, high in the mountains are the ruins of a monastery that once was the center of learning and instruction for some of the greatest leaders of Tibet. It once had over 2000 monks and on the mountainside are ruins of monasteries, schools, homes and stupas scattered across the mountainside as a reminder of the Chinese Cultural Revolution. But, the meditation caves are still there. There are some 87 caves on the mountain. Thinkers seeking retreat to meditate, hermits, teachers, political leaders, monks, and intellectuals have been coming to this cave complex for over a thousand years.

I climbed this mountain and in the back of a cave met an aged Tibetan monk. He showed me the relics from a former age that still survived in the back of his cave. He had been living there guarding those relics for over fifty years. I wondered about this man who had given most of his life, living high on a mountain in freezing conditions with few human comforts all of that time. He said that most of his time was spent in prayer and meditation. Fifty years of his life to preserve and protect those relics that he considered spiritually important! He felt a spiritual presence and was determined to live the rest of his life there. I said: "Why?" He then explained: "At one time this was a huge center of learning. There were over 4000 monks and a great intellectual atmosphere of study and development. It was all destroyed, except these few caves. I am here; to keep the memory of that time alive and in hopes that someday we will renew this place again."

I wonder and am in awe at the determination and discipline of the "hermits". Their experiences and lives are exemplary. One renowned Tibetan hermit limited his "practice" to watching his mind. He drew a black mark on the cave wall whenever a negative thought came. Initially his walls were all black; however, as he became more mindful, his thought became more virtuous and white marks began to replace the black ones. The Dalai Lama says: "We must apply similar mindfulness in our daily lives."

If there is anything the people of our time need to learn from Tibet, it is the practice, discipline and the power of meditation. In this world of daily pressures and fast moving technology, we seem to be immersed by fast moving ideas, images, and events…they overwhelm us. The more dangerous impact is that they numb us from thinking, meditating, and reflecting on our inner selves. Modern "activity" and distraction numbs us from seeing below the surface and keeps us from intellectual depth.

A monk went to the caves of Drak Yerpa to meditate, and he sat for 5 years. He did not eat much, rarely bathed, did not enjoy new clothes, he simply tried to pray and meditate and increase his intellectual and spiritual development. He was near the end of his pilgrimage, and was at a point where he thought he had attained a high level of spiritual development, when a woman came by. She was also on a pilgrimage. "Great monk, I am on a mission. My prayers have led me, through a dream that I must give a man of enlightenment three gifts…that is my life goal here." "What gifts?" he asked. "I must give a sumptuous meal, a glass of wine, and my body for love." She said. "Oh woman, go away, I have been here for years without those three things, and you tempt me. You will make me lose my merit" He said. She then cried and begged. "Please, please help me. Will you let me give you at least one of these gifts?" He thought about it, and said: "Well,

69

you may prepare a meal for me at sunset, and I will eat it prayerfully." So she came and prepared the meal and it was such a good meal, the first he had enjoyed in ages, and when he finished he thought. "You know, it would be a waste not to have a glass of wine to finish off this wonderful meal." So he drank wine. But on a full stomach and feeling the impact of the wine, he saw the girl, and now in the rays of the setting sun coming in through the cave entrance, she seemed so beautiful. He took her and they engaged in deep and vigorous sex for a long time. Afterwards, he said, "Oh, no, what have I done! I've lost all of the spiritual growth that I worked for 5 years to attain. Now I must start all over." And as she left him, he sat and prayed, and reflected, and began another long journey of meditation and sacrifice. But occasionally he would think, perhaps with a bit of guilt, but perhaps with a bit of wistful joy, of the meal, the wine, and the love he shared in that cave.

This story tells us something about life. Sometimes our goals and those of others may conflict. But sometimes even when we try to escape the temptations of the world, they follow us. But the story does not take away the importance of adding a little quiet and meditation to our lives. We don't have to find a cave, but we can find a comfortable or beautiful quiet place to think and meditate. Great spiritual leaders have done this for all of history. The Dalai Lama arises at 3:00 A.M. every morning to meditate. Billy Graham used to say he used the "before dawn" hours to pray and study. The great A.C. Bhaktivedanta Swami Prabhupada who brought the Krishna belief to America from India got up every morning at 4:00 A.M. Lee Goodman, a Christian millionaire in Texas is praying and meditating every day before dawn. My friend Bob Collier, a prominent businessman in West Texas is often up before dawn to pray and sing. Lee and Bob will tell you that the "meditation and prayer" time gives this joy, peace, and clarity of thought. The moments give the insights for business and relationships. It is possible that it gives them an advantage in their negotiations and dealings, because of the clarity and fore thought the process brings.

But if you are not an early riser, consider the mid day, or the evening for your quiet times. Who knows...think who may walk by your cave some day???

ASIA AND THE GLOBAL CITIZEN

Our cave has expanded in the new world. For the entire world has become our cave. This became apparent as I made my way through Asia. China is a land governed and dominated by the force of law and the force of soldiers. From there I traveled to Tibet, a land of deeply ingrained religious culture now conquered by China's army. From there I went to Nepal, where the poor mountain folk, tired of poverty, rebel against the royal kingdom and against concentrated wealth. The trip continued to India, perhaps the most diverse nation in the world, culturally and religiously. India is a nation contemplating war with Pakistan, and both nations have fingers willing to press their nuclear buttons. Epidemics such as SARS and AIDS ravage nations in this sector. How do the new Citizens of the global community deal with violence and social instability?

We recognize that each person generates a spiritual aura, an energy emanating around him. It can be intensified with love and focus, peace and compassion. Others can also sense it if they are attuned, and it can always make a difference in the world around us. We must focus more than ever on compassion, love, and peace. We must be facilitators of peace and understanding in every communication, every contact. We must be sources of peace and confidence. Others are drawn to people of confidence. The violence in the world represents something more than political failure; it represents the failure of institutional religious culture. Put bluntly, it represents the failure of the Church, the Synagogue, and the Temple. Millions around the world are deeply disappointed in religious leaders and are shocked and amazed at the lack of positive leadership of organized religions around the world in the face of devastating war, conflict and power mongering. Nearly all wars are energized by religious or political dogma. They require the emotion and energy that religious zealots generate to give political strength to the efforts. Communism, Islam, Hinduism, Judaism, and radical right wing Christians— all of them have failed to serve their believers and have failed the people of the world because they have not brought their energies and resources to bear to teach— indeed, to demand—their followers to follow the ways of peace. Many are cowed and intimidated into silence by political powers.

In the face of the failure of the religious institutions of the world and the imminent dangers of war that could kill not only hundreds, or thousands, but millions, it is up to citizens of the new global order to fill that vacuum with compassion and be that impetus for peace. If we can't take a lead as an organized gr)up, we should individually take steps to show the religious institutions how to regain that focus.

When religion all over the world allows itself to be manipulated by politics and by greedy or power hungry men who have anything but "religious" motives, great harm can result. We see this happening all over the world. In Afghanistan, we saw Al Qaeda and the Taliban manipulate their people into cruel and warring behavior. In Pakistan, we see Islamic clerics and teachers encouraging young people to hate and to commit their lives to killing Westerners. In India, we see radical Hindus pressing for nuclear war. In western China, we see radical Islamic people warring with the Chinese. In Tibet we see the devout communists of China using every means at their disposal to destroy Tibetan culture and religion. In Israel, we see political leaders calling for the salvation of the Jewish homeland by destroying Palestinian communities. In Palestine, we see radical clerics and leaders teaching children how to strap bombs to themselves and commit suicide and murder in their Jihad. In America, we see right wing Christians calling for a Holy War against Islam. And we see politicians calling on the name of God as they approve policies to war against other peoples. Again, it is worth repeating. When religion allows itself to be manipulated by politics, great harm can result.

Why don't religious leaders stand up in the face of those who would manipulate their religion in the name of politics or war? Thomas Jefferson argued that government institutions should be separate from religion and especially that politics should be separate from religion. He identified history's lessons that the mixture of religion and politics inevitably led to abuses. The new citizen believes in another approach, that religious institutions must not try to integrate themselves into government and politics unless the

73

people are 100% homogenous and in favor of it. Otherwise, minorities will always suffer. We see the mix of politics and religion as a dangerous and explosive concoction, like mixing gasoline with fire. The result will surely be conflagration and violence, pain and injury. One of the few exceptions to this basic premise has been Buddhism. Perhaps that is because the Buddhist religion is intrinsically opposed to aggression, war and violence. Furthermore, the Tibetan Buddhists who follow the Dalai Lama are perhaps the most homogenous culture in today's world.

Thus, the mixture of church and state in a nonviolent and peaceful people can work. But it is rarely accomplished.

CHAPTER SIX

☸ ✡ ☿ ☪ ✴ ⛩ 🧘 ॐ ∞ ☯ ✝

RELIGIOUS MONUMENTS TO ART AND MAN'S CREATIVITY

One of the truths of life and of all religions is that beauty, art and creativity lift us up and inspire us; they are one way of seeing the faces of God. What of the great religious monuments? Are they just brick and mortar? To the extent that they represent and are the result of order, logic, beauty, and balance, to the extent that they cause serendipity and joy, inspiration and awe, to that extent they become energy. To that extent they have a life. These buildings may be of common elements such as brick and mortar but they are also an investment of spirit, diligence, love, art, planning, discipline, and vision that creates something greater than the sum of the parts.

Thus the Potala in Lhasa, Tibet, emanates an energy and power beyond any age, country, or ruler. It carries with it the energy of the hands and spirits that built it and the energy of the generations of people who have blessed it, maintained it, and allowed it to inspire them to worship and pray. It says something, and it encourages something, and the world is enriched because of it. When such a place is desecrated or destroyed, the destruction diminishes us all.

Consider the largest building complex in the world, Angkor Wat, in Cambodia. Built a thousand years ago, it still fills people with awe. Art, beauty, architecture, order, logic, music: these are as near to the face and voice of God as most will ever see or hear. They are the best that some can experience in a life and world of conflict, confusion and delusion.

Consider the thousands, millions of man-hours over a period of 200 or 300 years that invested in the Potala. Consider the prayers, the dreams, the songs, the craftsmanship, the great art, the creativity, and the sacrifices that went into this structure. It enriches us all and is not lost to us with time. The passage of time seems to magnify its power and mystique, like the aging of a fine wine. As one professor of antiquities said, "These buildings and artifacts are not about brick, mortar, or copper; they represent the lives, culture, energy, history, and attempts of inspired people to communicate beauty. They represent life and beauty!"

Consider the Taj Mahal, built by the Mughal Emperor Shal Jahan out of love for his wife Arjumand. She had given the Emperor both children and love, and her death moved him to this "magnificent obsession." Through it, he tried to express his love with the beauty of the building. With that as motivation, every line, every piece of marble, every precious stone that was inlaid took on a goal: to express the beauty of love.

The Citizens of the new world order believe in, support and encourage these "magnificent obsessions." Indeed, consider the life of a person. How many people, when they die, leave nothing of lasting beauty or meaning, or significance? All the years they lived, they built nothing. They left nothing tangible.

We encourage every person to be a part of a "magnificent obsession," to build something of power, beauty, and positive energy that will stand and last long enough to be of meaning on this earth. A monument or building, park, lake, poem, song, painting, book, photograph or even a novel. Something to bless mankind. If a person is "called" or fortunate enough to be blessed with a "magnificent obsession" of creativity he must pursue it.

Consider each day a grain of sand, rushing through your allotted hourglass of time.

Do something with it.

Now this begs the question at another level. The institutional level.

IS THE SACRED AND MAGIC GONE WHEN RELIGIOUS INSTITUTIONS ARE DESTROYED?

In Tibet, there is something special when you witness a spot where the Chinese destroyed a stupa or a sacred religious structure and replaced it with a street or parking lot. The parking lot is not special, but when you witness thousands of prayer flags waiving all over and around and see people come daily, to what seems to our eyes, an empty spot, and to pray, and spin their prayer wheels it is as if the Chinese aren't there! It is as if the Red Army trucks passing along these roads and the soldiers don't even realize that they are passing under canopies of prayer flags or beside mani stones. When the Chinese built a disco and prostitution house across from the sacred Potala, it was meant to be a slap in the face of the Tibetan and Buddhist tradition. But 99% of the Tibetan people ignore the place. If you go in, it is largely empty. The only ones who go there are Chinese soldiers and occasional tourists. The Tibetans don't see it, don't hear it, it isn't in their spiritual reality. Instead of insulting the Buddhist path, it seems like an empty and corrupt gesture, one that has been made irrelevant.

The mystery and power of the Tibetan spirit and intellect prevails. The institutions are largely gone. The temples have been made into museums, with limited numbers of monks allowed. But the spiritual and intellectual power of the Tibetan religion now makes the Chinese effort in Tibet seem stupid and clumsy, scared and paranoid. The Tibetan people seem at peace, bound together by adversity and mutual struggles. The Chinese seem restive, tense, scared even to let tourists openly visit with Tibetans. What this teaches is that even if religious monuments and institutions are destroyed, people of faith and insight can still sanctify and revere the holy that is within our world.

INSTITUTIONAL CONFLICTS

Institutional traditions and conflicts sap the energy, creativity and purpose of mankind. They can be very confusing to people, particularly in the area of spiritual development. One might expect politics and conflicts, manipulation and negativities in the business world or the political world, but when it occurs in religious institutions, it can cut out the heart of the religion. Consider Tibet. This land from 1600 to 1949 closed its borders and adopted a national priority to research and develop inner space (also called the inner workings of the mind through spiritual development). Tibet wanted to protect and preserve its cultural and social integrity, and Buddhism was the institutional vehicle for this effort. The people of Tibet became what many believe to be the world's most devout and spiritually focused nation. The Buddhist institution and the political leadership became one through the Dalai Lama. The people were centered on a religious and social system that made compassion and integrity its central identity.

In 1949, China was a child of the new "Communist" World. They were enthused and zealous about their concept of a new secular society. This philosophy considered religion an evil and an "opiate" for the people. The atheist communists developed a system of thought that was also a religion. This system was intent on converting others to its ideology. It became a religion, and Lenin, Marx, Stalin, and Mao Tse Tung became its most revered saints. While in the Buddhist world every office displayed a portrait of the Dalai Lama, in the Chinese world every office showed a portrait of Lenin, Stalin, or Mao. Statues of Lenin or Mao were erected in every city park, and public buildings were adorned with their images. Thus the religion of Communism and the political leadership of the nation of China became one.

When China "liberated" Tibet in 1949, it clashed head-on with a culture of the exact opposite of political and religious institutional values. Temples were destroyed, and to this day the ruins still bear witness to the destruction of this era and the "cultural revolution" that followed in the 1960s. Monks were killed; hospitals and schools were destroyed. The largest medical school in Tibet was on a hill just across from the Potala, and it was razed and replaced with a Chinese radio tower. One has to wonder why anyone would destroy a medical school, a college, or an elementary school. But the Chinese did. China even called the language of Tibet "religious" and forced the children to learn Chinese instead of Tibetan in schools. It became illegal for Tibetans even to hold a photo of the Dalai Lama, but photos of Mao were considered special.

Fifty years later, consider the confusion of contemporary Tibetan youth. The culture of their parents and ancestors is frowned upon by the government. It is trivialized as being colorful and quaint, superstitious and silly. The new institutional government of China and its Communist religion is considered progressive and modern. The government of China systematically controls the media, education, financial institutions, hotels, travel, power, commerce—everything. It even bans foreign visitors from communicating with local Tibetans. Two vast institutional systems are sending out opposite signals, and Tibetan youth are conflicted. On one hand they value and see the power of their historical cultural systems. Yet, to survive and succeed in life, they must conform to a foreign institutional culture.

This type of confusion is eliminated by the culture of the citizens of the new global order. Why? Because they can focus on core ethical and global values rather than be chained to any institutionally mandated system. The Tibetan youth, for example, can appreciate and understand the teachings of compassion and enlightenment while still trying to understand the equalization promise and goals of Communism. One might ask if the Tibetans make this leap, what are they to make of prayer or mantras.

A song of the 1960s says: "Do you believe in magic?" The song asks the right question, especially when considering religious issues. Without magic, what is the power and mystique of religion? The answer for the global citizen is "Yes, of course I believe in magic!" We believe and recognize the power of prayer more than ever! We simply reject then notion that it must to be draped in institutional robes, whatever the institution. Do we reject the institutional robes? NO. We just don't need them as much as we once did. There will always be a place for religious institutions. The mystery, rituals, and traditions of institutional religion are the custodians of culture and art. They are too valuable to discard. We simply see that one can approach our concept of God or enlightenment without the necessity of going through the traditions and creeds of the institutions. The question becomes very basic. Can an individual approach God or enlightenment directly without the help of a cleric, priest, or monk? Yes! Can a cleric, priest or monk be helpful in a spiritual quest? Yes! But the core values are the central goal and the central power, whether institutional or individual.

CHAPTER SEVEN

ॐ ✡ ♈ ☪ ❖ 🧘 ॐ ∽ ☯ ✝

MEDITATION, SUFFERING, OBSERVATION AND LIGHT!

The importance and power of meditation is coming back into the forefront of medical research. Doctors now understand that meditation not only has mental and psychological benefits but physical benefits as well. Dr. Davidson did an extensive research study on Olympic level athletes and identified sections of the brain that could be identified by electronic means as centers of positive emotion. He found that the brain of a person, who was depressed or "down" emotionally, showed specific readings. But when that same person was taught to meditate on "compassion" that the centers of the brain called "centers of positive emotion" increased their readings by 800%. The negative readings of the depression disappeared or diminished dramatically. John Cave Sen researched the workings of the brain for years, and proved that patients afflicted with chronic illnesses, arthritis, asthma, even life threatening diseases, benefit from meditation. He teaches that patients who are taught to meditate for 30 minutes daily on mindfulness, compassion and positive emotions actually show an improved immune resistance to disease. The body produces measurable increased chemical antibodies that give the human body higher resistance to disease.

Meditation as a practice has been a part of the life of

spiritual seekers for all of mankind. Moses went up to a mountain, alone, to find the Ten Commandments that became the basis for two world religions. Christ went to the wilderness to pray. Buddha went to the forest to meditate. Native American Indians teach that each young warrior should go to the wilderness for his "medicine retreat" and meditate and pray until he finds direction, and his spiritual name. In the history of Christianity, meditation played a huge part of Christian life, through the 1600's, and then it seemed to gradually diminish. As the West entered the scientific age, meditation almost ceased to be taught as a daily Christian practice. Worship services evolved into a time of action, singing, prayers, sermons, standing up, repeating chants or prayers, and sitting and listening. But silent meditation all but disappeared in the spiritual world of most Western churches. But some traditions, particularly in the East, continue to see the value of quiet meditation, and this may account for the massive growth of Buddhism, and Zen in the West. For it again trains and allows the person to use his inner self, his mind, to achieve spiritual awareness, "highs", insights, and joy. My wife and I visited a church in Ft.Worth that employed a minister who was a student of meditation. We were surprised that the class was filled with people, young, middle age and old. They were an affluent and educated group. She led the group into a meditation time and the time was a relaxing and joy filled event. We first meditated on our breathing, the joy of breath and then our sensations throughout our body. Then we meditated on our concerns, and joys. Then we meditated on our families and our happiest moments. When she rang her little bell, to signify that the time was over, we had been there for over an hour, and it seemed like five minutes. Another surprise result occurred. When it was over, we felt refreshed, relaxed, rested, as if we had been in a long, peaceful sleep. It was a remarkable experience that taught me much. Now, even with the many demands of life, I try to make a time and place to "be quiet". It provides an added dimension and perspective to life.

REFLECTIONS ON SUFFERING AND PAIN

When asked what his schedule was, the Dalai Lama said: "I get up at three every morning and meditate, often considering why there is suffering and pain."

Buddhists believe that there is a logical reason for all suffering and pain. Suffering is always a result of some action. Christians vary on this. The "predestination" Christian belief is much like the Buddhist Karma belief that suffering is predestined. Other Christians believe that suffering is a result of bad behavior. But some people believe that suffering is simply a random fact of life.

Meditation can be a great aid in helping us begin to understand suffering and pain on a deeper level. Krishna teaches that we are essentially good but that suffering comes as a result of our mistakes and bad actions. Buddhism also teaches that we are spiritual beings - precious and good - but that our suffering is caused by "Karma" or the result of past bad actions. Buddhism starts with the statement: "All is suffering" and then builds on the concept that life naturally includes suffering and pain as the foundation element of existence, but that we can see enlightenment by prayer, meditation, and compassion, eliminating suffering in our lives and those of others. Krishna and Buddhism seek to increase the quality of life through appreciation of "the journey" while still seeking an ultimate goal of enlightenment.

Judaism and Christianity teach that we are evil in basic nature, and basically sinful in our essential nature, but that if we renounce evil we open a path through faith and good works to eternal joy upon our death. In their concept that God created all things, there is inference that in "love" He created the system that allowed this suffering, but it is because of a greater plan to motivate humankind to good works. The reward in these religions is focused upon the eternal reward of "everlasting life" at death.

Plato and Atheists teach that simple logic, and cause and effect are the primary causes for pain and suffering. But the elements of fate luck and random events can alter a life even though a man may be doing good things.

In all of these teachings, there is one common idea. Suffering and pain are a fact of life. It is hard wired into the programming of existence. A common response of great thinkers of history is that we can make positive actions our attempt to do and be good, and to improve ourselves as well as the world around us in spite of suffering.

But that is of little comfort to a mother grieving over the sudden loss of a child, or a survivor of a family destroyed by war or some tragedy. The question of suffering and pain continues to follow us, for no amount of intellectual pondering can eliminate the pain of life. But time and good will, kindness and compassion, creativity and beauty can act as balms for the suffering of life. The one aspect of suffering that may provide comfort is the fact that we all experience it. In that empathy we can share the pain, which perhaps is the greatest gift of all.

Meditation leads one to be "where you are" when you are there. It also leads to more careful observation. Our lives are so fast and cluttered that we often miss. An ancient quote from the Himalayas says: "Be where you are otherwise you will miss most of your life!"

EXERCISE IN OBSERVATION

Before we can experience we must observe. How do we look at things? Do we see what we look at? Critical to the ability to experience life fully is the necessity to "see". We do look, don't we? But our culture, the tempo, the demands, the stimulus of our environment, has an influence on how we look at things.

Here's an example of observation.

I'm sitting on a covered wooden porch, looking at the view high in the mountains of New Mexico. There is a vast mountain range, blue gray in color and above it white cumulous clouds idle against a blue sky. To see the mountain I must look through the branches of pine trees. It is cool, and I can smell the fragrance of the mountain forest. The clouds are always moving, growing, changing, from brilliant white against a pure blue sky to tones of gray. The shadows in the clouds give them texture and depth. If I lazy eye a bit, I can see faces in the clouds and think of the days when I would fly toward the clouds and clip a bit of cloud with my airplane wing. From this distance the clouds appear so calm, peaceful and beautiful with slow almost imperceptible movements. But in reality, the clouds represent violence, energy, hail, wind and lightening.

Looking at the clouds, I am actually looking through a forest of pine trees. They stand upright, reaching for the heavens. The branches move ever so softly with the mountain breeze. I see the pine needles, green, yet reflecting a bit of golden color as the sun hits them. At the tip of each branch is a clump of pine needles and at the tip of the clump, fresh bright young needles emerge out of an ochre bloom. The branches come out from the trunks of the trees, and they are a brownish gray. Looking more closely I see the texture of the bark, rough, curling up from the virgin wood below the bark. Looking still more closely, the tree trunk is very complex in surface texture. There are sections of white algae growing on the bark. It is at first just a clump of white, but upon closer inspection, it too has a texture, like bark, and it is not white but has subtle colors of blue and green, even yellow in it. There is a section of something that almost looks like green hair attached to the bark of the tree. But it is complex. The "hair" is actually tiny growing miniature branches, all twisted and turning into what seems like a "scouring pad" of nature. The tree trunk changes colors to a beautiful golden brown with tinges of reddish brown; this is where the old bark has come off. There are tiny ants climbing up the trees, exploring every little nook and cranny. The ants climb up to the tree sap, and there is one stuck in the sap. I ponder helping out and further wonder if I don't, will he become a treasure encased in a sarcophagus of amber some day long in the future; some piece of jewelry for people to admire. Inside of these areas of virgin brown wood is sap. When the sun hits it, it looks like honey. It smells fresh and pungent, like a mountain medicine, and to the touch is stiff and sticky. The more your work it between the fingers, the softer it becomes, and it changes to a white color, no longer translucent, and becomes so sticky it almost glues the fingers together. I touch the sap to my lips and it tastes like turpentine and smells like mountain ointment. I hear hummingbirds and mountain insects. I feel the cool mountain air and the sticky pine sap on my skin. I see so many things now, so many more things. I could sit here for hours and not see it all. I feel a sense of reverence and discovery, humbled by the complex beauty around me. And I thought I was just looking at a mountain.

WE ARE BLESSED WITH FIVE SENSES

Sight, smell, touch, sound, and taste. Not to mention memory, emotion, pain, and joy and, perhaps, senses that we have but cannot yet identify. We can train ourselves to use more of our senses for when we see more deeply, we experience more of life.

As we look at the workings of the world around us and see the events of mankind, we must "see" more of what we look at. We must see the workings of people and identify their agendas. When we speak to another human, read his writings, or hear his music, we must listen with more effort. What is he really about? What are the hidden agendas that might achieve harmful or good goals? We must learn to observe both the big picture full of perspective and the "tiny details" that can be manipulated and change everything. Look…and see. At this point when we begin to see, we can then appreciate light.

THE MAGNET OF ENLIGHTENMENT

On the "other side" of Mount Everest (the Chinese side)

there is an ancient Tibetan Buddhist monastery. It is located high in the mountains, and sits on the highest elevation of any monastery in the world. It is called the Ronbuk Monastery. One has to wonder, what attraction could bring people interested in spiritual growth, to locate there. Thin air, cold winters, harsh sunlight because of the altitude...Yet there it is! Access to it, is by an even higher remote mountain pass, called in Tibetan Changri-La. Changri-la. I wonder if the Western myth of Shangri-La originated at this place. And if so, it would make sense. For the Tibetans of that region are warm, enlightened, and it would be logical that they would have seemed like something of a "Shangri-La" type community to a Western explorer who happened upon them. It is no wonder that we are attracted to a "Shangri-La". Throughout mankind's history, man has been pulled toward religions as if by a magnet. Sometimes religion creates the opposite effect as well. Sometimes it pushes people away especially when the religion is mean spirited or judgmental. But, there is an undeniable urge on the part of mankind to seek religious inspiration, to find logical systems to achieve a higher ethical and logical level...to find, if you please, enlightenment.

In the 1960's I saw it in the eyes of underground Christians in Yugoslavia. Then, the country was still "behind the iron curtain". I remember smuggling Bibles into Zagreb, and quietly hiding them in the back door of a home there, where people worshipped secretly to avoid persecution. I saw it in Mongolia, and Cambodia, and Kyrgystan, where people lived in places that they could be persecuted by other groups, yet they longed for a religious connection. In Northern India, a young child wrote me once and said: "Will you baptize me?

I've studied and heard about Christians and want to be baptized." The next time I visited India, I made a special trip, and baptized that young girl...it was a childish request, yet sincere, and filled her longing for a religious connection. I traveled to China, when it was under strict control of the Communists, and worshipped secretly in the homes of people all longing for religion. In 2002, I traveled to Tibet. There I saw a nation ripped apart by religious persecution, and saw the commitment and devotion of Tibetans to pray and worship in their own way. I saw them unashamed to pray in the streets in public and in full view of the Chinese who had pressed so much destruction on them and their country.

There is an attraction to enlightenment, almost like a light draws moths at night. People are attracted to the light. But, sometimes the institutions that are built around the "light" dim, or hide its view. Sometimes the light is changed to be garish, invasive or punishing. Some religious people distort the light and turn it into a harmful force. It is this alteration of the light that concerns children of the new global generation. They want to see the light, not a colored or changed, or interpreted, or controlled vision. They want to see the pure light, and let it shine on their lives. They want to gain enlightenment that is not corrupted by humans.

In Alaska, the winters are such that several months of darkness last until a sunrise. There, when a business or restaurant or meeting place turns on the lights, people are attracted to those places. They become so oppressed by the darkness of the light, they will go to where light is. But, if the light is shut up in a building, where they can't see it or easily get to it, they don't go so freely. Thus it is with the magnet that draws us to enlightenment.

CHAPTER EIGHT

ॐ ✡ ☥ ☪ ✴ 🧘 ॐ ✝

DIVINE SERENDIPIDY

Perhaps it might be better called a state of spontaneous creativity. It is a manner of life and action that requires that one be in emotional, spiritual and intellectual balance. It is a manner of living each day with a sense of wonder, curiosity and courage. It is a special state of mind where one is in the "zone". Carl Yung called it "Synchronicity" or "An event going beyond mere coincidence that makes you believe that there is some deeper meaning."

I discovered divine serendipity by accident which is logical since serendipity suggests "a surprise that delights". On a trip to Mongolia, I encountered a young Buddhist monk at Erdun Du, the great capital of Mongolia of the Chinghis Khan at Karakarum. It is a remarkable place, at one time capital of the most powerful nation on earth. It is a difficult twelve-hour drive by 4-wheel drive out of Ulaanbaatar, Mongolia. There wasn't a paved road to it and often we found ourselves driving across the prairie and crossing streams as we followed the dirt road. Sometimes the road would just dissolve in deep ditches and then divide into several trails across the Steppes. The way to Karakarum does not have gas stations and the only food was at an occasional roadside "Gher" or round tent where a woman would cook up some fresh killed mutton and serve it with Aura (fermented mare's milk).

But if you are ever in Mongolia, the trek to Erdun Du is

well worth it. For there at the location of the great Khan's kingdom is a great wall of stupas perhaps a mile square. The wall is 20 feet thick and 30 feet high and every 50 feet or so is a stupa. Inside the compound are Buddhist temples built from the ruins of the Khan's compound. It is a most mysterious and marvelous place to visit.

It was there that I met Lama Sodrig. This young monk was standing near the center of the compound and I gestured that I would like to take his photo. He told my interpreter that he gave his permission if I would then send him a copy. I agreed, took his address and his photo, and 2 months later sent him a copy from the United States. This was the first of a series of letters in which we shared the stories of our lives. One day I got a letter from him inviting me to meet him in India, to meet His Holiness, the Dalai Lama. I showed it to my wife who encouraged me to go. At the time that seemed to be a problem because I didn't know how I would afford to pay for the trip. A couple of weeks later in a visit with a friend with the World Bank, I asked him about India. "I'm thinking of making a trip there, have you ever been?" I asked. He replied; "If you are going into that region, the World Bank could use you to teach a banking and economic development symposium in Mongolia. We'll pay your expenses and a per diem." Suddenly my trip to India became a financial possibility! So I traveled to Mongolia and was in the process of teaching the banking symposium there when one day I got an envelope from the U.S. Embassy marked "URGENT MESSAGE". In it was a fax from my wife with a copy of a letter from the manager of a Buddhist monastery in India on behalf of Lama Soderig that had been mailed to me in America. It said: "Sorry to inform you, but Lama Soderig is no longer in India because he left for home on personal business. He cannot receive you but you are still welcome to visit us."

I looked at the letter. Lama Soderig was no longer in India, he was in Mongolia! What a coincidence because that is where I was! So I took the long trip to Karakarum and started walking around the great compound and asking: "Where can I find Lama Soderig?" After a number of curious responses to this strange American, someone got the message and said they would take me to his home. A short time later we walked up to a Mongolian Gher and there was Lama Soderig. "What are YOU doing HERE? You are supposed to be in India!" he said. "What are YOU doing HERE; you are supposed to be in India too!" I replied with a smile. It was one of those times of spontaneous creativity. We laughed and shared stories as Lama Soderig's mother and sisters cooked us a simple meal of baked mutton, with sliced cucumbers. It was almost unworldly sitting there in a Mongolian Gher, as they sliced the meat from a side of lamb, and roasted it over an open fire in the center of the "Gher". Imagine that all of this happened because of a series of events. First a photo, then a promise, then a letter, then a symposium, then a grand reunion in a remote place. From that moment I determined to live every moment on that trip with spontaneous creativity. It took me to Japan, China and India where I met people and experienced "serendipities" that provided insights of life, love and humanity that deepened my understanding and life experience.

Spontaneous creativity requires not only a balanced mind and spirit, but also the openness to the situations and direction that life can provide if you are ready. When I've been able to get to this state of existence and have allowed it to work the result has almost always been one that I call "divine serendipity". Experiences of joy, wonder and even awe have been mine.

In society we put shackles on ourselves. Like a mule pulling a plow in a field, we put eye blinders on to keep us from looking either way. We are taught and told to simply plow the row straight to the end and never to stop and look around at the possibilities life affords us. We miss so much of the color and texture of life when we keep our heads down looking only at the "assigned" row we must plow. When we can get into the "zone" and see all the human beings around us, we can join with fellow brothers and sisters who are spiritual beings with our common emotions. Then we begin to see a different dimension of life. If we allow ourselves to "go with" the flow of life in a spirit of curiosity, love and good will, it can take us in the most profound directions.

One day I was in the Beijing airport. It was a busy travel day but the airport was particularly disorganized that day because of a labor strike and work slowdown. Authorities locked all of the internal travelers in a secured area and we were stuck there for several hours waiting for our flight and waiting for the airport personnel to get back on the job. As I sat in a room with several hundred other people, I began to study the people. One man was well dressed in a dark suit with a brief case and an assistant. His body language seemed to suggest authority. Another tall man with a multi-pocketed travel vest exuded charisma. I approached the "authority" man and said: "Well, we are stuck here together and we may as well make some positive use of the time by getting to know one another. My name is Ben Boothe from Fort Worth, Texas." He looked up with surprise, hesitated a moment and gave me his name. He was the Ambassador of China. He said: "I've never had anyone do this before but it is most pleasant". He and I visited for a while and it was a positive experience for both of us. Later I approached the "charismatic" man with the travel vest. "Where did you get that vest?" I asked. He smiled and said; "I got mine on Park Avenue in New York, where did you get yours?" This started a friendship that continues to this day. That man was Demir Yener who at the time was in charge of development of World Bank programs in Asia. Demir and I both went with the "flow" of creative spontaneity and the resulting relationship has taken us to nations throughout the world. I believe that the economic symposiums to help nations develop their economies internally to be more effective in encouraging peace and goodwill and accomplishes more good than 10,000 soldiers with tanks and guns could do in the same nations.

Divine serendipity or spontaneous creativity is a rich experience. It is a powerful way to open up your life to new experiences. It is explosive with power because humans are so scared and timid. We live in a world where people are organized and structured to jobs and rules of behavior. When we catch a glimpse of positive energy that is love based with only positive motives, it seems to open new vistas of living and joy. People come alive when they are allowed to "take the blinders off". Of course there has to be a basic premise, a foundation concept of ethical respect with the idea that: "I am here only for positive reasons and only to contribute and experience something good".

I am blessed with special friends who come from a Christian tradition. They define their life style in the traditional "guided by prayer and the Lord's direction" philosophy.

One is Lee Goodman, who is a business executive in Fort Worth, Texas. I was Lee's banker and watched his financial fortunes grow to the tens of millions of dollars. One day Lee told me: "I live every day, trying not to get in the way of the Lord's will. I work to remain open to his guidance." Lee and many others live their lives seeking and experiencing divine coincidence. These are spiritual connections. Some might call it an energy field. Some might call it a "rapport" with humanity. Some might call it a divine direction. It is not an energy or experience limited to any one church, religion, group, belief system or person because no individual or group can claim to exhaust all of the spiritual possibilities. It is an experience available to all if we can get on the right frequency and into the zone. Find your "serendipity" and go with it. While you are looking, let me suggest three potential "primer" journeys.

INTERESTING SPIRITUAL JOURNEYS AROUND THE GLOBE

1. FAITH: In Japan is the great Zenko Temple of the Tendai Buddhist sect. In Nagano, up among the central mountains is a temple complex. At the Temple there is a steep dark stairway in the main hall that leads down into a passage running beneath the central shrine. One gropes along, in absolute darkness, turns two corners, and under the "holy of holies" one's hand is guided by a long depression in the wall to a key. When you touch the key it is supposed to have some miraculous quality. Then one pushes on past two more corners in the same stygian darkness, and clambers up another stairway, gradually into the light. The experience is an act of faith...blind faith. The journey through darkness into light.

2. MEDITATION: In the book: The Life of Buddhism (U. of Calf Press, @2000), there is a description of a meditation experience by Taiko Yamasaki. It was penned in 1955 from the Mt Mison Temple in Miyajima, Japan.

The Morning Star meditation originated in China in the year 717 C.E., and Yamasaki got permission to do this meditation of chanting a mantra while looking at the morning star, Venus. There Taiko Yamasaki tells his experience: "At the beginning I suffered pain in my legs from long hours of sitting, making meditation difficult. Gradually my mind and body came into harmony and I then felt lightness and tranquility. During my meditation, my body came to feel almost transparent, while my mind and what I saw around me were clear, like crystal. Far from being a hallucination, this came from increased clarity of consciousness, as though I had come to a place where heaven and earth join. As I walked, and left the hall, the sense of the vastness of the universe would remain, as though I were seeing the world for the first time. The trees were no longer separate from myself, but seemed a part of me, as thought we were a single being. Although my emotions were involved, this was not an experience of ordinary sentimental intimacy, but rather an experience of consciousness, a realization that one is made of the same substance as everything else and that nothing in nature is unrelated to the self. At night I would go up to the mountains and meditate in the open, feeling the stars in the late Autumn sky surrounding me on all sides, as thought I were hanging in space. This sense of unity with all things remained in my mind even after the practice ended after I returned to the world. A profound feeling of gratitude and a new appreciation for life came to affect everything that I did.

It would seem that meditation opened up a new dimension of spiritual awakening for him. Something deeply needed in this modern, pressure bound world.

3. NATURE: Assisi, Italy, is the home of Saint Francis of Assisi. He was the father of the Franciscan sect of the Catholic Church. A visit here in the springtime with walks through the flowers of the Easter season is a beautiful lesson of growth and renewal. Here one can find spiritual exploration of one with the beauty of nature. It is said that St. Francis was so gentle that birds would eat from his hands. The followers of Francis made positive contributions to development and spirituality throughout the world.

4. HARMONY: In this world of religious violence there is a marvelous example of religious harmony and sharing. Sodnaya, Syria has a rich religious history. Christians were there early and built a very old Church building. But after the Christians had dominated the area for hundreds of years, Islam began to grow in the area. In Sodnaya, instead of fighting and killing each other, Christians and Muslims came to a peaceful solution. The Church became both a church building and a Muslim temple. One half of the building is used by Christians, one have by Muslims. Every Friday, Muslims gather to worship and pray. Every Sunday, Christians gather to worship and pray. They differ in religious preference but are a shining example of harmony to the world.

CHAPTER NINE

ॐ ✡ ♆ ☪ ✺ 🧘 ॐ ⸾ ☯ ✝

ADDICTION OF THE WEST

You and I may be addicts. This is an age of addicts. Webster's dictionary defines an addict as; "to give assent" "to give oneself up to a strong habit". What is your addiction?

If you want to have some fun, go to a friend and ask what his addiction is. You may be surprised at the things he brings up. I did this with a successful business executive recently with a response of discomfort and then a litany of things that I didn't expect. William Bennett served as Secretary of Education for the Reagan Administration and was an advisor to several Republican politicians. He then went on the television circuit and wrote several books about morality, family morals, virtue and unfortunately his writings took a strong political slant. One book spoke of the "Death of our Age" referring to Bill Clinton as morally corrupt. Then, in May of 2003, Bennett was forced to admit that he, the champion of "virtue" for the right wing of American politics, squandered $8,000,000.00 (yes, million) dollars in a gambling addiction. Thus, the old adage that "one who lives in a glass house shouldn't throw stones" comes to bear. No one is perfect, and the more judgmental people are, the more likely they will be judged. "Judge not that you be not Judged" says the Biblical sermon.

But there is another addiction, the one you and I share.

It is the "addiction of acquisition". Particularly in the Western culture, we feed on the temporary "highs" of consumerism and acquisition. Housewives tell of the STYD syndrome ("shop 'til you drop"). This is a popular method of eliminating boredom and depression. Men tell of the "high" and "elation" they feel when they buy a new car, a new tool, gun, house, or investment property. The feeling is temporary and the need for it grows and grows. It is an appetite that recurs, always larger than before. It drives the "consumer" economy.

After 9/11, there was an instant and dramatic drop in consumer spending in America. People wanted to be home with their families, they wanted to consider more important things. They pulled close to their loved ones. The President of the United States then made a speech and encouraged Americans to "shop" as a patriotic duty, to support the economy. In fact, the Western economy is dependent upon the addiction of acquisition, and encourages it in multiple ways. Social standing, personal habits, continual marketing, all encourage "acquisition" and "consumerism".

I, for one, admit that I am an addict. I have bought airplanes, cars, houses, apartment complexes, land, farms, all-terrain vehicles, sporting equipment, boats, commercial property...and every time I have experienced that momentary "high". My wife loves to buy clothes, jewelry, and things for her house. Over a lifetime it has become apparent that the elation of acquisition is temporary. Often after the "high of acquisition" comes emptiness, the realization that acquisition is not the deepest method for inner peace.

There are arguments that suggest, convincingly, that as

happy people we should simply enjoy the "blessings" of affluence and laugh, play, and enjoy the toys that we can afford. I have no argument with happiness, and have enjoyed my share of "toys". But it becomes ever more apparent to me, that we must work to see that we are not enslaved by "things". We must own them, and not allow them to own us. I've heard others suggest that they have acquired wealth and "things" to enjoy, and justify it with the argument that they plan to give it all to charity when they die. I have no argument with that. Many churches, colleges and heirs greatly benefit from the shared "acquisitions" of others.

FOUR QUESTIONS FOR REFLECTION AND DISCUSSION:

1. Does your addiction bring you and or others joy and peace?

2. Is your addiction motivated by love?

3. Does your addiction cause pain to others?

4. Does your addiction cause pain and suffering to you?

There is another way, represented by people who can be happy with a simple lifestyle. They have shunned the "Addiction of the West" and have opted to search for their "highs" in different ways. Some ways are meditation, study, compassion for others, personal reflection, art, writing, creative endeavors, building ideas, or things of depth and importance.

It is hard to break an addiction. It is hard to even create a desire to do so, because we enjoy the momentary high so much. But addictions generally are expensive, and impact other aspects of our lives. Consider your addiction.

CHAPTER TEN

ॐ ✡ ♆ ☾ ✤ 🧘 ॐ ✶ ☯ ✝

CONFLICT, RELIGIOUS VIOLENCE, JUDGEMENTALISM & VIOLENCE VS PEACE AND LIFE

In 1996 at the Summer Olympics in Atlanta, Georgia, thousands of happy families were enjoying the biggest event in the nation. Then suddenly the crowd was horrified by an explosion that killed one and injured over one hundred people. It was a random act of terror. Who could do such a thing? Five years later in the mountains of North Carolina, Eric Robert Rudolph was captured. His profile released by the F.B.I. explained a great deal. "Rudolph was believed to follow Christian Identity, a white supremacist religion that opposes abortion, homosexuality and foreigners."

He represents what this chapter is about and is an American example of the 'dark side'. This chapter deals with conflict, then discusses judgementalism that leads to violence. After that, perhaps we can better appreciate peace and precious life.

The new religion of the global generation repudiates religious violence. The first terrorists, the Assassins of Persia, planted seeds of violence in religion. In the year 1225 A.D., the most powerful man on earth, with the greatest army on earth, Chinghis Khan, put forth a decree that the terrorist assassins should be killed. He sent forth his Mongolian army into Persia, and after 20 years of battles and slaughter, they managed to destroy all of the castles and forts, but history has shown that religious and political terrorism is almost impossible to eliminate. Religious fanatics of nearly every religion have their history stained with the blood of religious violence. After the Assassins, there were the Christian Crusaders who went to conquer and kill in the name of Christ. History tells us that although their official targets were Muslims, they often killed Jews, Orthodox Christians, and anyone who happened to be in their way. History is replete with religious wars, fanatical murders, and terrorist acts perpetrated by Hindus, Muslims, Jews, Christians, and by hundreds of sub-cults or smaller religious groups. Some religions, almost as a tradition, utilize the Jihad, or Holy War, as justification for violence. A vivid example of fundamentalist violence is the conflict in the Islamic world. Kevin Bales, in his book; *Disposable People, New Slavery in the Global Economy* reported from Pakistan;

"In this Islamic Republic, where a state religion has tremendous power, religious leaders have little interest in working together to bring harmony. Running parallel to and interpenetrating with family blood feuds are the ongoing wars between Islamic factions and sects...mosques with divergent interpretations of the Koran duel with loudspeakers attached to their towers. All day and night the supercharged sound systems boom out prayers and sermons vilifying their religious opponents and calling on the "faithful" to shun or even attack them...in one area a series of insults chalked onto a wall led to a battle lasting ten days. Communication was cut off as the two sides hammered each other with mortars and rocket launchers...the death toll was over 200...a constant stream of assassinations takes place as the groups target each other's leaders...six or seven mosques are bombed each year. Because Pakistan lacks an effective state education system, militant sectarian groups have established their own schools. In the single state of Punjab there are over 2,500 of these *deeni madressabs* or religious seminaries...there are 219,000 children, mostly male, in these schools...there is no shortage of young boys to instill with suicidal religious fervor."

In the Islamic world there is ongoing war between moderates and fundamentalists. The mindset of fundamentalism often leads to violence, whether it is Islamic, Hindu, Jewish, or Christian. Unfortunately, the war of logic, reason, and sanity against fundamentalist radicalism is a global war for all thinking people.

Some political leaders, as a last recourse to buttress their power, evoke religious zealotry to gain support. History tells us the story of Chinghis Khan going to a mountain to pray and staying in his tent for 3 days. When he emerged he announced a "Holy Direction" to conquer the world. Kings, dictators, prime ministers and yet even presidents have evoked "God" or "Allah" (or whatever deity is at hand) to justify their wars and to whip up support from simple good hearted religious people to fight and die and pay for the wars. In almost every war of the 20th century, the "opponent" has been characterized as "evil", and religious prayers and support from "God" to destroy the other side are evoked.

104

One of my formative experiences as a college student was during a visit to Germany where I stumbled upon a beautiful cemetery for Nazi soldiers. The headstones included the Christian cross, prayers and tributes to them for their service as good Christians, killed in battle. Before that moment, it never occurred to me that German soldiers that we had fought and killed in war considered themselves Christians too! That they prayed to my God and that religiously, we were brothers. I thought that they must be evil because they were on the "other" side. Subsequent to that day, I have circled the globe many times and have found spiritual people in every culture, every religious tradition. People far removed from my own culture and traditions have impressed me as deeply connected spiritually with unique and valuable insights. One of the most remarkable men I have met is Shantilal Somaiya. His friends include the Dalai Lama, the Pope and religious leaders from nearly every tradition. Shantilal Somaiya's father owned a vast sugar empire in India and one day he announced to his son: "I'm going to devote the rest of my life to study and helping others. You take over the business!" When Karamshibha Somaiya died in 1999 he had established several colleges and numerous charitable humanitarian institutions. I met Shantilal Somaiya in June of 2003 while speaking about the emerging regligion of the global generation at the Indian Merchant's Chamber in Mumbai. Somaiya is an engaging man who literally kidnapped me to show me his colleges taht now teach some 26,000 students. A devout Hindu, he now devotes his life to study and good works. He said: "We are like a glass dipped into the ocean. The glass is our personality but when it is gone we are still water—a part of the spiritual energy of existance." He believes that all religions are to be studied and revered. To that end he has established colleges to study Hindu *Vedas*, Buddhism, Jain, Christianity and many others. "The hope of the world is in teaching that religious people are on a common quest for enlightenment—not a quest to destroy one another." he told me.

When I hear from these people like him, I realize that there are religious, and spiritual people from other traditions, sometimes they are more spiritual than leaders of my own cultural church roots. Thus the evident fact is that we should not judge one another because we are brothers in the global community of seekers...if we will allow ourselves to see the spiritual side of all people. When we see that, perhaps we can realize that we can do away with religious violence, religious terrorism, and religious wars.

In the Christmas of 2002, I was visiting Lubbock, Texas. On one street, some of the houses were decorated with beautiful lights and images. A man built a nativity scene in his yard, and then there was a sign. I walked close to read the sign expecting it to say: "Merry Christmas, Peace to You". Instead it said: "To the God forsaken thief who took our baby Jesus, you are the worst kind of low life. **God will get you!**" It was so inappropriate. I walked up at first feeling joy in the beauty of the display, but upon reading his sign, I felt angry at him for writing that sign. It was strange that the anger he felt was spreading out with his sign, and then I felt angry with him for taking away the beauty of the walk and evening. I could see how the youngsters in that neighborhood would sense his violence and want to harass him just to get a rise out of him. But then I felt sorry for him. He missed the point of the season, of the lights, of the very nativity that was in his yard. Instead of spreading love, he was spreading violence.

If such a small event as that could make me feel angry and violent, how much more powerful is a murder or war in the name of religion? The negatives spread like pouring gasoline on a wild fire. Negativity, warring in the name of religion is a powerful and dangerous force to be feared and handled with great care.

THE DARK SIDE: 5 EXAMPLES

1. "Berserker" is a Scandinavian concept. The word comes from the historical background of an ancient Norse warrior in a frenzied rage. The history of wars tells us that in every war, there are incidents of soldiers "snapping" and going berserk. They go into a violent and destructive frenzy, often killing, and torturing at random.

It is true, that even as every human is endowed with "light" and goodness, he also has a "dark" side. One of the "berserk" projects of WWII was Japan's Unit 721. Unit 721 of the Japanese government was located in Manchuria under Japanese occupation from 1939 to 1945. It was conceived and managed by Sharo Ishi, a man some believe to be one of the truly evil and cruel people in history. His unit was conceived to experiment on live humans to develop chemical and biological weapons.

In this compound, he took Chinese people off of the streets, sometimes at random and used them as guinea pigs for experimentation. No person who entered "721" ever left alive. The scientists of "721" documented their experiments in detail, and included:

- Handing out chocolate candies laced with poisons, to watch how Chinese children died

- Air dropped fleas, infected with "plague" on random villages, to see how effective it was in killing people

- Froze people alive, or froze limbs, to study how best to treat frost bite, and how to design protective clothing for Japanese soldiers

- Dissected people alive (the concept was to inject them or infect them, and then cut their stomachs open and observe how the internal organs reacted

- Bombed villages with anthrax, germs, and chemicals and then followed up with teams who cut living people open to observe their internal organs

- Created blimps to float across the ocean to drop bombs and incendiary devices on the USA and developed "ceramic" bomb covers to hold anthrax and other agents to drop on the US from these high altitude balloons. Some of their experimental balloons actually reached America but did little damage.

At the end of 1946, U.S. scientists and the CIA recommended that Ishi be protected and his "fellow researchers" be treated as colleagues. Ishi and Japanese scientists gradually translated and gave the research to the USA. Ishi and his scientist were given immunity in 1948, much of their research was transferred to Biological Labs in Maryland to help them research chemical and germ warfare on behalf of the U.S. government.

2. Tuol Sleng and the killing fields of Cambodia. I have

visited the areas in Phnom Phenn, Cambodia, on the outskirts of town where the "killing fields" of Pol Pot are. In the late 1960's and early 1970's, thousands of people were tortured, beheaded, disemboweled, in an attempt to change the culture of Cambodia. There is a monument of skulls, 70 feet tall, and the pits of mass graves can still be observed. When I was there in 1999, I saw human teeth that had been knocked out of people's heads lying on the ground. There is a prison compound within the city called Tuol Sleng. It was managed by a soldier of Pol Pot who became a fanatic murderer, named Douch. He chained people to their beds and never released them. They were simply tortured and starved to death. Others were tied by their feet, and lowered into barrels of human feces. At this compound, they were photographed, documented, and systematically killed and tortured. They were electrocuted and then placed in a "torture bathtub" used for suffocation. Douch also used a cage of spiders, centipedes, snakes and scorpions to terrify people. They used hooks, bludgeons, whips and knives. Their photos still hang from the walls of the buildings. It is one of the "darkest" most evil places in feeling that I have ever visited. On the wall is a grotesque map of Cambodia made of human skulls of victims. While visiting this place, I felt the physical presence of evil in Toul Sleng.

3. I have visited Dacau, Germany, where similar compounds existed for "medical research". In Dacau the gas chambers burned day and night, and it is said that Germany, ultimately killed 3,000,000 Jews during WWII. Many of them were burned or gassed alive in Dacau. People there were frozen, injected and generally used as fodder for human experimentation before they were killed. One of the most touching photos is one of

naked couples sitting outside in an open air experiment to see how long it took them to freeze to death as they embraced one another.

4. In Iraq in 1992, it is said that Saddam Hussein authorized the "chemical gassing" and chemical warfare on the Kurds in the north. Environmentalists report that the area, 11 years later, still suffered a high rate of birth defects and population with distorted and wounded bodies.

5. 9/11. This event sponsored by religious and political fanatics murdered over 3000 civilians and horrified the civilized world. The grief and shock then turned to national anger when a few weeks later it was answered not by a selective "police action" but by a world wide "War of Terror" by the United States Government. Thus, we learned that violence begets violence...terror begets terror...anger begets anger.

6.   In 2002, and 2003, the US government, in its "War on Terror" unleashed military forces on Afghanistan and Iraq, with bombing, missiles, cannon, and a myriad of military actions. Why is this relevant to this book? Because in this environment, these actions have specific religious implications. The radical attacks on Americans are driven by the energy of angry and radical religio-political philosophy. Furthermore, the American responses to this war have been endowed with "religious" zeal, the U.S. President first referring to his military efforts as a "Crusade" and his repeated references to prayer. Furthermore, a large segment of America's religious Christian right has adopted an attitude that this is a Holy War, and they are invested with the concept that almost any actions are justified to

"save Israel". Strangely, in the language of the world, killing during war is not considered murder or even inhumane. Sometimes we must wonder what part of the Biblical commandment: "Thou Salt Not Kill" the religious and political leaders don't understand. In a gruesome display of human nature, people throughout the world were glued to their T.V. sets to see the latest video of smart bombs blowing up buildings. What the world seemed to forget was that this was not "make believe" or entertainment. With every one of those bombs, with every video of another "smart bomb" people were killed, dismembered, terrorized. The American people were not allowed to see photos of the terror they poured upon Iraq and Afghanistan. The torn bodies and tormented families were never seen by American viewers. But, Reuters and other media showed some of the tragic images. Two images that stand out were a man weeping over the coffins of 15 family members. He lost his wife, children, brothers, sisters, and mother - all civilians - in one American attack. There was another photo of an Iraqi child who lost both arms, blown off by an American "smart bomb". We might caption the child's photo, "created by God, mutilated by Americans".

In Iraq over three thousand civilians, including women and children were killed by American bombs. Those with tender hearts were confused and depressed by America's action. Otherwise generous and sweet spirited people were placed in a position that suggested that to be considered "patriotic" that they must support a war that they didn't necessarily want. War begets war, and terror begets terror. There is no doubt that the religious implications of this war and the anger generated in response will cause even more religious violence around the world. And yet, the confusing matter is that Americans are not cruel and violent as a people. In this case, they were being led and told what to do by a leadership that was elected by a minority of Americans. This again reminds of the power and implications of voting and the power and implications of nominations to the court systems. This can be instructive to people throughout our globe.

The dark side exists. We have to come to grips with the fact that the dark side is in all of us. It is in every person, every nation, yes every religion. As I now see it, the truth of the matter is that when nations "Pray for our troop's victory" they are equally praying for the murder and destruction of other peoples...who as Mark Twain said; "Are also praying to God for the same thing". God must think us all dark, beastly and a little insane. This is a compelling call for those who "think" and for those who "care" for humanity...the children of the global generation, to invest energy to help bring sanity and clarity to the world. The graphic vision of the brutality of man, of the "berserker" quality in mankind has one good side. Perhaps by its very awful nature, it can teach us something about ourselves, and teach us, drive us to a compassionate life.

JUDGEMENTALISM AND REJECTION, REFLECTIONS AFTER A CONFRONTATION

I called this story: THE SPIRITUAL SIDE OF JECKYL AND HYDE after a disturbing, but typical meeting with a fundamentalist that illustrates the banal side of fundamentalists.

It was his eyes, yes the eyes

A vacant, intense, mean look
The eyes told much more than the voice

I was hapless and as innocent as any sinner, going about my life, working dawn to dusk and then some. I thought my life was beyond such childish dealings with fundamentalists after endless journeys around the globe searching for beauty and insight in remote and ancient places. I came to believe that helping a few people improve their lot in life was worthy of my sweat and treasure.

So I created an import business to create a market for the goods made by those who couldn't join the global economy. With the help of Tibetan partners, we opened a showroom in the USA. To those poor and simple people on the other side of the earth I said: "Send me the fruits and creations of your hands. Send me your art and your crafts and I'll buy them and sell them for you!" The thought was that it would help them to feed their families and let them retain their dignity. My sweat and treasure was thus vested in others. It was an investment in people. This seemed to me to be worthy of my time and treasure.

Alas one day a preacher named Jeckyl, (or was it Hyde, I don't remember), came by to "buy my breakfast". As I chewed his eggs, the question of what he wanted flowed around my mind. Or rather, how much he wanted! For I've never met a preacher who bought a meal without attempting to extract a thousand fold more of the cost of the meal from my wallet! Young in my career as a banker, my ancient and wise mentor taught me a timeless truth.

"Avoid the 4 P's. They will take your money, break your heart, and rarely repay or give anything of lasting value back"

The 4 P's. I pondered as I swallowed the last of his eggs. I remember two of them were Prostitutes and Preachers. I recall asking my mentor, "Which of the 4 P's is the most honest and the least business risk?" "Prostitutes of course" he snorted "At least they tell you how much up front".

Alas, my host was a preacher.

After the eggs and toast and endless chit chat, he finally said: "Well a minimum gift of $5,000 is required if you want to stay on our saints and directors list." Plus you need to sign this document called a STATEMENT OF FAITH. It is our way of verifying that you are of sound faith. It assures us that you that you agree with us about which ones are going to heaven and which ones are going to hell." To his chagrin, I didn't commit but simply kept eating breakfast and making light conversation.

Then his eyes hardened, bored and glared. They seemed to scream out. It was the scream of a man who knew his craft. He knew how to use honed skills of motivation by the sword of guilt, intimidation and rejection. His eyes were like those of an angel of wrath and judgment.

He realized that I would not give him his precious $5,000 or his statement of faith so he pulled out another weapon. "In your shop I saw a statue of Buddha. This bothers me for in my church they would dis-fellowship you for this." Here was the Jeckyl and Hyde transformation; a man of God turned now into an angel of judgment. "You can't be a true Christian if you keep those icons" he shot.

He made me angry. "My despicable little man. You are an embarrassment to your faith!" I said pressing my finger to his chest. "People like you bring down your religion. It is people like you who exploit and enslave millions while self righteously giving them a Bible. It is people like you who declare war and then kill in the name of your God and country. People like you who trust your little system of law and virtue and then impose it on others before you would feed a widow or help a child. People like you who preach love and hospitality and then practice dis-fellowship and rejection. People like you who broadcast fire, hell and judgment and draw circles to keep others out rather than taking the needy in. People like you who crucified your savior in the name of self righteous indignation. It is all in your eyes."

Those Jeckyl and Hyde eyes seemed to be fiery with rage as I left him standing at the restaurant.

I returned to my office still agitated at this small minded little man. The agitation came from letting someone like him get to me. In the quiet of my office I read a story of a famous Christian evangelist. He had given his life to teaching others by his acts of love. In an airport there was a prominent Buddhist Lama who devoted his life to helping others in love. They recognized one another across the airport lobby. But they didn't speak the same language or did they? They sat beside each other and held hands together and smiled at one another. Theirs was the language of love and unity. They spoke without uttering a word, understanding the deeper language of shared love, shared life goals, shared efforts to help humanity. As I thought about them, my agitation drifted away.

UNINVITED VIOLENCE

I was on Freeway 635 North, of Dallas, Texas. Interstate

635 has twelve lanes, six going each direction and still becomes almost grid locked during evening rush hour between 5 p.m. and 6 p.m. every weekday. I was driving an Isuzu, with a front bumper guard, and making about 65 miles per hour. That is all that the traffic would allow safely. I was in the left hand lane, the passing lane, but in that traffic, it made little difference because no one was passing anyone. The key to traffic driving is to blend in and try not to get hit in the rear or try not to hit anyone in front.

Suddenly, a red sports car driven by a young man sped around my right side. He pulled dangerously close to me as he cut in front of me. He didn't miss me by an inch. Then as he got in front he immediately crashed on his brakes. I was forced to hit my brakes hard to keep from ramming him. I noticed he was looking in his rear view mirror and gesturing in an unfriendly way. I slowed down to let him go and he then hit his brakes again almost stopping in mid traffic. This time I hit his rear bumper.

He really started gesturing then. He wanted me to stop but I was on crutches and thought it too dangerous to stop in those six lanes of traffic so I pulled to his right and told him that his bumper was ok but I wasn't going to stop. He was furious. He nearly caused a bad wreck in his determination to stop me. He pulled in front, slowed, sped, pulled to my side, and he rode my back bumper.

I was the recipient of uninvited violence. I remembered the numerous cases in Texas of road violence and how several people were shot every month due to this type of anger. I tried to ignore him and this man followed me for over 30 miles before we finally separated in traffic.

That experience caused me to ponder about how we can deal with unexpected violence that comes our way in our daily lives. I learned years ago that one of the most disarming things to direct at an angry person is a smile and to reach out and offer to shake hands. A compassionate demeanor, with the symbolic "I'm not armed" gesture of reaching out sometimes confuses and defuses some people. When I ran for U.S. Congress, people of opposite political persuasions would want to be angry and fight about this issue or that issue. I tried to smile and be kind to the worst of demagogues. It was very effective and it often diffused the violence.

In the broader world, Diplomats tell us that negotiation, communication and refusal to personally insult or make dis-respectful comments can keep nations from going to war. That is the diplomat's way of grinning and offering a hand out. We watched political leaders such as the arch anti-Communist Ronald Reagan become friends with the arch anti- Capitalist Mikhail Gorbachev because of a warm and friendly communication style.

But even with all of the love and compassion that we can muster, there are still some people so energized by hate and anger that they will do damage to others. In these cases it seems that the role is to be strong, and to assert strength but with dignity. A few weeks ago, my wife and I paid a visit to confront tenants that were several months past due. They were cursing her on the front porch as Paulette told them that they would have to move if they would not pay. Hearing their insults aimed at my wife I hobbled up to them (I had a broken ankle at the time) and told the young man; "You are going to apologize to my wife." He said: "I'm not going to apologize" I said: "You are going to apologize because

117

you are a man, she is a woman and you are better than to act like this." He apologized. The odd thing was that he was muscular and could have beaten me, a 54 old man on crutches, easily. But "moral persuasion" and my presence brought him around. Better to lock the door and not let uninvited violence in. But if it arrives, try to diffuse it with love, kindness, strength and presence of mind. This leads us to think of peace.

PEACE AND THE GLOBAL GENERATION

"If you do it to the least of these children, you do it to me" Jesus Christ.

PEACE. What a controversial word. Christ is called the Prince of Peace. U.S. Presidents have made a point of calling themselves "workers for peace". Even generals have called themselves "Peacemakers". One of the Bible verses that I was taught as a child was: "Blessed are the peace-makers for they will be called the Children of God". Yet, contrast that with one of the most popular guns of the U.S. West in the 1870's, which was called the "Peacemaker". The idea being that it was appropriate to use violence, even murder, to obtain peace. Those who demonstrate for peace around the world are often viewed as radicals, members of fringe groups, hippies, or even communists. This I don't understand, because Communists don't have any better record on "peace" than any other political group. One would think that those demonstrating for peace would be the most spiritual, the most devout, the preachers and religious leaders. Yet the prominent religious voices in the West have been largely silent. Those in the East have been vocal, but for violence. How have **they** forgotten the lessons of peace that all religious leaders teach?

In the 1200's, crusaders invaded the Middle East in the name of the "Prince of Peace" and called themselves apostles of peace. The United States and other nations have invaded and warred upon smaller nations, in the name of "peace". China has liberated nation after nation in the name of "peace".

So, where do we, the informed and supposedly "connected" generation, stand on "peace"?

We believe in peace. With the exception of a few radicals, nearly every sane person on earth will say that he believes in peace. Every mother who has birthed a child and every father who has raised a son or daughter will favor peace. But...it seems that in the real world, when push comes to shove, there are those who are more prone to violence than peace. We are better at fighting than loving, better at attacking than negotiating, better at reacting with violent action than with intellectual process.

Hindus teach peace, yet the papers tell of Hindu's burning Muslims and Christians in religious conflict in India.

Muslims teach peace. Yet in the past 20 years, Muslim fundamentalists are the source of more wars and conflict than any other people on earth.

Jews teach peace. Their Ten Commandments forbid killing, yet, look at Israel, not only is Jerusalem an armed camp, but every month a new conflict seems to rise up with Israeli tanks and jets firing upon another village.

Christians teach peace, and yet one reads of Christians in Northern Ireland killing one another in political and religious conflict. In the U.S. Christians bomb abortion clinics, claiming war on the doctors who run such medical services for women requesting abortions. The Christian right fans the flames of war in the name of God and country.

Buddhists teach peace and yet look at the violence that overwhelmed Tibet when the Chinese ran over that little nation. The Dalai Lama has consistently taught that the only way to deal with the abuses of China is through peace and negotiations.

Chinese Atheists teach peace, and yet every nation that borders China lives in apprehension of Chinese invasion. While the Chinese Communists teach peace, they historically have been brutal, particularly with religious people who also teach peace.

Consider the peace demonstrators. How many peace demonstrations have ended up in violence, street crimes, and arrests?

In spite all of these conflicts, when I discuss peace with individuals on a one on one basis, I find reason and hope. It seems that the group dynamics of politics and propaganda to the masses is largely responsible for putting us in "violent" mode.

Thinkers of the world want peace. During times of peace, people can best prosper and grow spiritually and intellectually. Societies can organize, buildings and developments go forward, and hope for the world can live. The new global generation believes in intellect, wisdom, thoughtfulness and yes, peace.

But the questions come. Peace at any cost? The question

is filled with conflicts. What if an armed maniac invades your house, threatening to kill your wife and children…do you simply sit there and smile and tell him that you believe in peace?! What do you do, if you have great intellectual ideals about peace, but you find yourself confronted with a mindless mad-man? Do you stop him if he can't listen to reason and to negotiation? What do you do? The answer is wrapped up the word, do. DO…It is a word of action. I hail from Texas. It is a place where people DO. Many Texans settled and made a life for themselves by being people of hard work, and action.

The question arises then, when you are dealing with people who are playing by an entire different set of rules, how do you react? That is why governments, institutions, even religious organizations such as the Vatican, have elite groups of trained and armed guards. To keep the peace. To protect and defend against those who cannot or will not live by a rule of law and peace.

There is an ancient story of a man who joined the army. He was a good man and approached the Buddha and said: 'I am appointed by the King to enforce his laws and to wage his wars' The Buddha replied. "He who deserves punishment must be punished…Do not do injury to any living being but be just, filled with love and kindness." Later on, one of Buddha's fellow teachers said: "All warfare in which man tries to slay his brothers is lamentable. But those who are involved in war to maintain peace and order, *after having exhausted all means to avoid conflict*, are not necessarily blameworthy" Speaking of a soldier who had gone into battle Buddha said: "if he moderates himself and extinguishes all hatred in his heart, if he lifts his down-trodden adversary up and says to him 'come now and make peace and let us be

121

brothers' then he will gain a victory that is not a transient success...the teaching of conquest is not taught to destroy the lives of others but to protect them...the person whose mind is free from the illusion of self will stand and not fall in the battle of life. He who harbors love of truth in his heart will live and not suffer, for he has drunk the water of immortality. So struggle courageously and wisely. Then you can be a soldier of Truth."

I was speaking to a banker in the Middle East, of the Islamic faith, and asked him if he believed in Jihad (Holy War). He said yes, but in this way. "I believe that we all have a war within ourselves. It is the Jihad. If we can fight and win this war within ourselves...the war to overcome the evil impulses, and to replace them with impulses of goodness and love, then we have won the Jihad. Ultimately, this is everyone's Jihad."

So, what is our stance? We believe in Peace. Historically after man has exhaulted and exhausted himself in war, he then tries to turn to something greater than himself to find peace. The most ancient of all established religions, Hinduism has a legend about the role of God in peace.

> "There once lived a mighty demon named Gada who, intoxicated with his prowess on the battlefield, continued to wreak havoc on all humanity. Finally it came upon Vishnu to provide succor to harassed mankind. Famed universally for his valor, Gada was equally known for his charitable inclination. It was said that he wouldn't refuse a boon to any individual however unreasonable the demand may be. Vishnu approached Gada as a Brahmin and addressed him thus: 'If you are so generous can

you give me your bones?' Gada immediately tore open his body and pulled out his bones. From these bones the celestial artists (Ribhus) fashioned out a mace for Vishnu. Thus striking two birds with a stone, Vishnu acquired for himself an invincible weapon while at the same time gaining respite for the world."

It is in honor of this demon that the mace is still referred to as 'gada,' in Sanskrit."

Thus in this story, we are shown that the God Vishnu exudes compassion, and used his wits to find a way to gain relief for mankind. The story is to teach us as individuals to have "compassionate intellect" and to use it in support of peace. Perhaps the ancient legend also teaches us to be more cunning and clever than those who create war. We are compelled to be students and intellectuals who will study, question, and debate peace. We will call for peace during times of war, we will urge leaders to think, to process, to negotiate...always with peace in mind. We will avoid the rule of mobs, and the rule of emotion that tends to cause people to respond to acts of violence with even more violence. We will avoid the temptation to be caught up in the emotion of "religious frenzy" or "blind patriotic emotion" that is sometimes manipulated by warmongers to gain massive following. We will not be manipulated by stories concocted to show the "enemy" as being less than human, thus worthy of destruction. We will know, sadly, but with wisdom, that there is cruelty, and darkness in each of us, and that our goal is to transcend that and seek out the compassion and light within each human. We will encourage people to ultimately consider their own "Jihad" and to seek inner peace. Then their attitudes regarding conflict, war and violence, will change.

When 9/11 occurred, there were a few voices in the world that called for patience, compassion and wisdom. Richard Gere, the actor, spoke in New York Central Park before thousands, and when he said that this was a time for "compassion and wisdom" he was booed by the crowd. At that moment Americans were mad, they wanted some kind of revenge. Some peace rallies were organized, but they were poorly attended, and the U.S. media gave them little coverage. But the voices calling for action and revenge were stronger and the US declared a global war on terrorism and promptly bombed Afghanistan back into the 19th century.

It is now known that specific planning to invade Iraq began just a few days after George W. Bush was inaugurated. Moreover, the PROJECT FOR THE NEW AMERICAN CENTURY written in September of 2000 outlined the creation of a "global Pax Americana", suggesting American domination of Iraq, Afghanistan, and other nations in the region. Thus the "war on terror" or the fear phrase "weapons of mass destruction" are now known to be arguments put in place to justify actions and policies that were already underway. The day after 9/11, Defense Secretary, Don Rumsfeld, sent a memo suggesting that government leaders use 9/11 as an excuse to invade Iraq. Thus, after all of the violence and the "war on terror", when the dust settled, the U.S. still had not captured or destroyed those responsible for 9/11. But many Americans, waving their flags and having seen the "smart bombs" explode on T.V. felt better. The cartoon, Doonesbury commented: "From now on the answer to every question is '9-11'".

During the same time, millions of Americans lost jobs because of a poor economy but they didn't seem to mind, for they were "at war". "9-11" was a good enough answer for their suffering. The U.S. President, rather than being a worker for peace, worked for war. Every president has a legacy and a skill that he is known for, and it appears that Bush is to be known as a warrior. The U.S. President sent out signals to all in his government to find reasons to war on Iraq. It should not surprise the American people that intelligence agencies came up with poor information, in light of the pressure from government leaders put on them to produce something. Political observers said that the 9/11 event, gave definition to the Bush Presidency. An international economist with the Ghandi Institute in India told me: "Without the war, would Bush have been considered a below average president, in a poor economy, with only mediocre leadership qualities." Political leaders throughout history have learned that wars bring political strength. This happened with Bush, pulling his polling figures to high levels. Interesting that in his case, it took war and violence, to increase his political security. Further it is ironic that much of his political support for the war came from religious groups who had been manipulated into thinking that it was "God's will" to go to war.

During all of this, most people of the world remained quiet instead of proposing moral, ethical, and philosophical questions on peace. There were few effective voices that could bring America to see that it was not acting like the world's leader for peace but rather for war. A few people worked for peace, such as Jimmy Carter, Bill Clinton, George McGovern and Kofi Annan. Finally, when millions around the world demonstrated and raised their voices for peace, they were ignored as their efforts were too little and too late.

Those who believe and practice the new religion of the global generation will be willing to stand up, and ask the hard questions. Those are the questions that cause world leaders to look inward, to see what they are doing and to realize the precious value of peace. The value of peace is the value of life.

PRECIOUS LIFE

Life is precious and in the global age, the age of movement, masses, dehumanization, and a globe teeming with billions of people; that life - individual life - has lost its value to some. Buddhist texts refer to life as extraordinary and precious, the result of an "enormous accumulation of virtue". The Dalai Lama says: "Why is it of such value? Because it offers us the greatest opportunity for spiritual growth: the pursuit of our own happiness and that over others. Animals don't have that ability to pursue virtue the way humans do."

The concept that life is precious, ironically, but not surprisingly, comes not from man's secular traditions. It always seems to come from religious teaching. Left to secular man...human life would be of no value or meaning whatsoever. It is religion that reminds us of this...teaches this, and gives you and I the concept that we are special, important, and worth something.

The implications that this idea has for war, social and cultural order, and our personal lives are mind boggling. Mark Twain's poem, the "War Prayer", tells the story of a nation at war and the people all gathered in a joyous ceremony at church to pray the boys off to war. The poem tells of an ancient man, an angel of God, who walks in and announces that God has heard "Both" prayers; the spoken one for victory and the unspoken one. He tells them that when they pray for victory in war, that they are also praying for the death and destruction of others...praying that families will be "torn to shreds" and "their blood- paved paths be filled with sorrow all of their days". Then he says, "The Almighty has heard both of your prayers. He awaits your decision as to whether he should grant your prayers." The poem concludes with the comment that the congregation thought he was a crazy man because none of his comments made sense.

CHAPTER ELEVEN

SOCIO-ECONOMIC IMPLICATONS

The philosophy of the global generation suggests that we take responsibility for our actions. It also suggests that people matter. The socio-economic implications are profound because there are powerful forces in the world today suggesting that institutions are more important than people, rigid rules and regulations more important than compassion and respect, and giant macro-trends of greed and power for a few at the top echelons of power are more important than the masses of humanity.

We see it in trends of the economic world to "bigger is better". Small family businesses throughout the world have been systematically destroyed in favor of global business. Small family farms have been destroyed in favor a giant "agri-business". Small communities have been disadvantaged by a world socio-economic culture that encourages migration to metropolitan hubs, leaving the small communities poor and crippled. We see it in the destruction of cultural, historical, and ethical systems. We see it as "culture" is destroyed and replaced by homogenized systems of economic greed.

In my economic work for the World Bank working in third world nations I devised the following "Cycle of Deregulation" that can be instructive.

Deregulation leads to consolidations
Consolidations lead to concentrations
Concentrations lead to monopolization
Monopolization leads to globalization
Globalization leads to de-humanization
Dehumanization leads to social
destabilization
Destabilization leads to Re-Regulation
Consider where your nation or your community is in this
cycle.

Look at history. In the 1900-1929 eras, massive
economic expansion took place without regulation,
leading to abuses, consolidations of small businesses
into concentrated power centers. This lead to giant
monopolies that expanded until they created
international influence. The global economy of the
1920's would have worked except it also allowed abuses
of power, and suddenly children, women, and workers
began to revolt because they found themselves terribly
exploited. De-stabilization began when the Great
Depression hit. Finally political pressure forced
governments to regulate to assure the people that this
kind of economic abuse by giant business wouldn't
occur again. Remember, regulations are typically put in
place to protect people from abuses. Gradually, over
time as regulations in the 1970's through the 1990's were
removed, we saw more and more small businesses fail.
They were being destroyed or "consolidated" in favor
of growing monopolies. This brought about global
giants that replicated the deregulation and consolidation
around the world. To the shame of the economic giants,
the global economy made the wealthiest wealthier, as
the number of billionaires doubled and tripled. But the
middle classes and lower classes found their incomes

shrinking. Then even their jobs were gradually phased out, as "middle managers" of industry found their ranks shrinking.

An executive of one of America's largest corporations told me: "The biggest change you will see in American business over the next generation is the elimination of 'middle management' jobs. Those people will be laid off". Statistics show that this has come about, and the trend continues to accelerate. But, the "dehumanization" that comes when over 1/3 of the world's population makes less than a dollar a day, and another 1/3 of the world's population finds that even though qualified and educated, jobs matching middle range skills are no longer there. What happens to these people? They have to start over again, sometimes at terrible pain and sacrifice. But the real tragedy comes to light when it is revealed that the top 2% of the world's population makes more money than ever, at the expense of the middle classes and the poor. Certainly, the de-humanization leads to anger, loss, and social destabilization. If a man can't get food to feed his family, he will eventually become violent against those mega-wealthy people and companies who have disenfranchised his economic stability and personal dignity.

The children of the global generation must see the broad socio-economic picture, and realize that in an enlightened economy the values of loyalty, support for workers, executives and families are of critical importance.

We must find ways, and there are many, to bring financial security back to individuals. One is to re invent small communities and allow them the hope of financial growth. Another is to support small family businesses, and entrepreneurs. To create an environment that will allow entrepreneurs to have a chance...a chance to realize their dreams and not be forced to be a puppet employee of some giant mega-corporation.

The reason for this is simple. PEOPLE MATTER. HUMANS MATTER. Business, government, religion, and politics are supposed to exist to help people, not the other way around. We need to find a way to re-center the focus where it should be.

An economic legend tells of a machine that was designed to consume the minerals and vegetation of the earth. That was its fuel. As it began to move across fields, it grew and became more powerful...more powerful than even the people who created it. Soon fences wouldn't stop it, and as it rolled across the land, it destroyed fields, crops, houses, animals, and people. It consumed anything in its way. There was no "political" control. There was no "ethical value system" to control it. There was nothing but the urge to "consume". Soon it was evident that the monster was out of control. It needed to be "regulated" in a matter as to make it productive, but not destructive. The metaphor is a good example of unbridled, totally unregulated economics. What history has taught us is that an economy that is totally without regulation is a predatory system.

For example, when I first visited Outer Mongolia years ago, there was only one paved highway that went across the country. It was only two lanes wide and was totally de-regulated. Guess who controlled the road in a totally deregulated environment? The big trucks! As they came barreling down the highway, cars simply were forced to drive off the roads to avoid being run down. But the total lack of speed limits, and highway signs, and patrol officers eventually led to anarchy. The road was often left in gridlock. Eventually everyone lost because of the lack of regulation.

In America, some people brag that we have an "unregulated capitalism". But part of the stability of the American socio-economic system is that we do have a regulated system. The banking system is regulated and protects the economy. The financial system of Wall Street is regulated. The cities, states, and even the highways are regulated. Yes, back to the highway metaphor, we all say we "hate traffic cops"; until we see a drunk, driving a speeding truck, then we are grateful for "regulations and traffic cops". It is the same in an economy. A totally unregulated economy always leads to the abuse of the "biggest and most powerful" to the loss of the small businesses and small communities. A system with balanced regulation protects the people, levels the playing field, and keeps us from anarchy and economic gridlock.

My friend Krishna Bahadur Kunwar is an executive with the Agriculture Development Bank of Nepal. He wrote an excellent book called: THE HIMILAYAN POVERTY, THREAT TO THE WORLD. In it he tells the story of concentrated wealth in Nepal. How that most of the wealth is controlled by a few people. He describes how corruption and bribery have thwarted efforts of world social organizations to help. His premise is that if we don't help the poor of Nepal to achieve a better life style then war and turmoil are sure to follow. The Maoist violence of Nepal is a perfect example of hopeless poverty taking action through anger and violence.

Other examples abound. While in Guatemala I learned that 92% of all of the land of Guatemala is controlled by only 5% of the people. The vast majority of the population is poor peasants forced to work as tenants on tiny tracts of land that they don't own. Guatemala also has a history of the poor rising up in anger. While there, I ate lunch with Rios Mont, a former President of Guatemala. While he was in power, his army decided that the peasants were Communists and they swept through the mountains of that tiny nation and massacred over 200,000 of the indigenous Indians. Mont has been labeled as one of the world's most vicious leaders by world human rights organizations. Yet when I spoke to him, he was charming and pleasant. He told me that he had no knowledge of or control over what some of his commanders did. But the fact remains that where there is wealth, greed and lust for power on one side and poor people on the other, eventually anger and violence can arise.

Sociologists and world economists have a great concern about the concentrations of wealth globally. With over 33% of the world's population making less than one dollar per day and a growing pool of people who were formerly considered in the middle classes becoming unemployed, there is much negative potential. How will people who cannot feed their families eventually react when they see enormous wealth gained at the expense of the middle class and the poor? Thus there is tangible need for a balanced system of socio-economic justice and opportunity.

All of this carries with it the underlying foundation of thought that people are important. A new socio-economic system must be the order of the world. We know Communism did not work. It was a good example of over regulation, over planning, and poorly conceived control systems. Totally free un-fettered capitalism with no regulations brings the abuses of the Enron's, Arthur Andersons, World Coms, and eventual abuse by the giants.

133

There is a system I call ELIGHTENED CAPTITALISM that recognizes the human need for rules, for government and for regulations that are carefully thought out to protect, and provide opportunity for people. It accepts capitalism but also provides proper structure to protect people. Remember, people are what it is all about. The global generation will help define this new type of economic system, and the world will respond with long term stability.

If we do not take responsibility to define this new type of socio-economic system and communicate it effectively, we will see the continuation of negative world trends that ultimately lead to a system of anarchy and eventual closing of world trade, communication and commerce as we now know it.

Consider, for example the trends that we have seen since 9/11 and the long term implications for the globe.

1. Total freedom and deregulation of the travel system and air training system led to the abuse promulgated by the 9/11 murderers. They entered the USA as students and took flight training with little or no documentation to authorities and then were able to use the freedom of our culture to hijack and fly the airplanes into buildings.

   RESPONSE: The responses of the American government have often been poorly conceived and poorly executed. Immigration has been limited. Students of foreign nations have been sent home by the thousands. Air travel has become so security oriented that millions of travelers have stopped using air travel all together. Airlines have been required to cut back flights and lay off thousands while flying has become less efficient, more expensive and more restrictive.

2. The governments of the world, led by the West encouraged free trade. The dismantling of rules and regulations allowed trade to flourish as the walls came down with fewer regulations, customs and tariffs. A new understanding of the family of the world expanded.

   RESPONSE: As competition has flourished, even good laws and regulations intended to protect people have been eliminated. The very instigators of free trade have been the leaders in challenging free trade by other nations as they attempt to export to the USA. Trade conflicts in international courts have created protective and vindictive attitudes. Thus in some cases nations have quietly begun putting up regulatory walls and trade and tariff barriers. These are taking the form of legal restrictions, regulations, tariffs, environmental regulations, duties and other barriers in response to inequities. Walls have begun to go back up. Is the era of free trade and global economics about to change?

3. Security and Customs were deregulated to lubricate the free flow of economic activities in a Free Trade, unregulated world of commerce.

   RESPONSE: The world since 2000 has seen customs and security become so cumbersome that some ports around the world report backlogs, goods stacked on piers, and ships anchored for weeks before the goods can be 'downloaded'. Importers report increased examples of crates being opened, equipment and merchandise being damaged or destroyed by 'customs' inspectors with a cursory note: "Please understand this damage was done because of the war on terror, or for security reasons". As a result, international importing and exporting has become less profitable and the timing slower and less efficient. In May of 2003 the U.S. government announced that a new cumbersome interview process would be initiated to people visa applicants will have months more delays, plus, those applying for political asylum will be incarcerated upon entry until their paperwork is completed through a process that could take years.

4. Wars and pre-emptive strikes are now a new and verbalized policy of the United States. The USA always owned the moral high ground, a political statement that the USA would never be the "aggressors", unless first attacked. Now, the USA has adopted a philosophy that it can attack any nation "first" that might someday become a perceived threat.

RESPONSE: Nations in sensitive areas such as India/ Pakistan, Israel/Palestine, the Balkans, Russia with political rebels, or numerous African nations, now have "justification" to attack any enemy they can define as a "terrorist" enemy. The world has become more war torn and dangerous now than in generations.

5. The USA insisted on attacking Iraq because it thought Iraq might someday get nuclear weapons. In the process, America was embarrassed that the massive supplies of weapons of mass destruction were not found. However, it ignored North Korea with a far larger army and confirmed nuclear missiles.

RESPONSE: The message to third world nations was that America might not attack or "invade" if you have nuclear weapons. Thus, a new race to develop nuclear weapons as a preventative measure from "liberation" by the USA or other nations may have been stimulated by US policy.

6. Religious moderates and intellectuals did not effectively speak out in the face of fundamentalist radicals, of Islam, Hindu, Christian and Jewish faiths.

RESPONSE: As a result, fundamentalists gained political power in the United States and numerous Islamic nations, and became more aggressive in Hindu India, and Jewish Israel. The world is seeing the fruits of less religious tolerance, and a radicalization of politics in many places on earth.

7. Politics and religion were homogenized around the world, with political leaders believing it made good political sense to align with religious leaders.

RESPONSE: Throughout the world, more examples are rising of political entities using government power to achieve religious aims. Therefore, while the abuses of a Taliban in Afghanistan were considered horrible to many, now it is becoming more politically correct to use government in "main stream" nations to achieve religious goals.

8. As nations have allowed political leaders to try to rejuvenate political, cultural, and social uniformity, we have seen nations like America, Germany, India, and Israel make statements like that of an American foreign policy adviser to the government who stated that "America is not a melting pot. It is supposed to be a land of white, Anglo Saxon, Christians. Others are not

American, because America is not the United Nations".

RESPONSE: Less tolerance, less multiculturalism, less understanding of the brotherhood of nations and the brotherhood of all people around the world has resulted. The incidence of violence on those of different ethic or religious backgrounds has increased. There has been manipulation of patriotism and religion to suppress, persecute and punish those who are progressive or open thinkers. History reminds us of the ethnic cleansing in central Europe, the bigotry of Germany in the 1930's, the Marxists of Europe, Fascists of Italy, Communists in Russia and China, or McCarthyism in America. All of these "regimes" used "patriotism" as the emotional catalyst for the social repression they foisted upon their people.

9. Faxes, telephones, and internet communications were all considered great tools of communication and freedom. Internet use was totally non-regulated with no standards or rules of service. When the Soviet Union was falling apart, an American diplomat commented that no dictator can survive in an era of free communications. Thus the West promoted vast communication advances and made them available at low cost with little or no regulation so the masses could afford them.

RESPONSE: As the world has become more totalitarian, governments have engaged in electronic jamming, listening, monitoring, and even electronic warfare to limit the free communication throughout the world. Part of this has been as justification of the "War on Terror" and part as a means of national political institutions gaining more power over the people in their nations. In China, internet cafes have been closed down and internet activities closely monitored. In the USA the government has been given more power to tap phone conversations, and nations around the world have expanded their electronic surveillance departments. It has been said that no conversation on a telephone and or fax or e-mail is now private.

10. Governments, in response to "terrorist" attacks, devised a policy-response of "war" authorizing attacks, assassinations and imprisonment as the ultimate solution.

RESPONSE: Historically, as Winston Churchill said: "A nation can never win a war against terror, because it is a war against ideas." Thus with every bomb or killing of a "terrorist", a dozen more are born. Governments would do better by dealing with the root causes of the various "terror" movements instead of multiplying the violence by use of violence.

In short, we now see a world with the following characteristics that have evolved in recent years.

1. HIGHER UNENPLOYMENT. More people are now unemployed than at any time in history. The world's leading economy lost over 2,000,000 jobs between 2001 and 2003.

2. HIGHER UNDEREMPLOYMENT. More people who are educated have menial jobs below their qualification and skills than at any time in the earth's history.

3. HIGHER LEVEL OF POVERTY. More people on earth

(estimated at 30% of the world's population) make less than $1 per day.

4. MORE WARS. The world is a more violent place.

5. MORE TERRORISM. Terrorist activities have not declined but have increased since the "War on Terror".

6. MORE UNCERTAINTY IN SOCIETY. People throughout the world are concerned about their personal, physical, and economic security.

7. FUNDAMENTALISTS RADICALIZATION THROUGHOUT THE WORLD. Fundamentalists of every religion and social order are becoming more radicalized. Christian, Hindu, Islam, Political Right and fringe groups seem to be energized by the uncertainty of the world.

8. ECONOMIC DESTABILIZATION AND DECLINES in every major nation is increasing.

9. LESS TOLERANCE FOR DIVERSITY abounds. In Germany and France, people are hostile to immigrants. In India there is less religious tolerance. In China, more persecution of different religions abounds. In America, a post 9/11 social movement of intolerance attacks everything from singers, actors, politicians and even businessmen who dare to question or criticize political policies.

10. THE RULE OF FEAR AND DISTRACTION. Government leaders throughout the world are using fear and distraction of tragedies and war for political purposes to control their people.

11. LOSS OF INDIVIDUAL LEGAL RIGHTS. Governments are following the U.S. example by voiding the rights of legal representation and holding some without due-process-of-law in the name of the "War on Terror".

12. LOSS OF PRIVACY RIGHTS. Governments are allowing greater espionage on private citizens throughout the world. It is now said that any internet, telephone or fax communication is subject to be monitored by someone.

13. THE COST OF DOING BUSINESS IS HIGHER due to increased security costs.

14. TRAVEL IS MORE DIFFICULT AND LESS EFFICIENT.

15. CITIES, STATES, AND GOVERNMENTS HAVE HIGHER COSTS DUE TO INCREASED SECURITY MEASURES, CAUSING WIDESPREAD TAX INCREASES.

The world has not been a happy place over the past three years.

These are a few examples where a deeper dialogue and intellectual analysis by those with a broader vision could have resulted in policies that benefit humanity rather than punish humanity. These are specific socio-economic examples of ways the "global generation" through intellectual discourse and analysis can help the world by wise input and effective communication to policy makers.

CHAPTER TWELVE

ॐ ✡ ♆ ☾★ ❋ 🛕 ꣳ ✺ ☯ ✝

THE CONNUNDRUM OF PURNIMA, THE FLOWER MERCHANT OF MUMBAI

I first saw Purnima before dawn on a sidewalk in Mumbai, India. She represents the challenging socio-economic and moral problems that good people must deal with and solve in our modern world.

I was staying at the Ambassador Hotel next to the waterfront and it was my habit to arise before dawn and go for a walk along the ocean. Purnima and her family were asleep on the sidewalk. She was lying on her back and her baby crawled onto her, raised her blouse and was nursing. Purnima was so exhausted that she was completely unaware of it.

The scene touched me. They were obviously poor and the cut flowers they sold to tourists and passers by were knocked over beside them, on the piece of cardboard that served as their mattress on the hard sidewalk.

Later in the morning I walked back out to the corner. There she was selling her flowers with a baby in her arms and a little girl about 6 years old helping hand the flowers to customers. Her husband was standing in the middle of the busy intersection trying to sell flowers through the windows of cars as they stopped for the signal light.

I introduced myself and asked: "Where do you live?" She smiled and said: "Oh sir, we used to have a farm with a house and animals. There we grew ample food but the government built a dam and flooded our farmland. We lost our home and with no place to go we decided to move here. This spot on the sidewalk is our home. We pay the police 100 Rupees to let us sleep here."

At the time I was working on a consultancy for the World Bank in Asia. We were proud that we financed and planned massive infrastructure projects to help developing nations. I knew of a giant dam project in India that meant to provide hydroelectric power. But here, I was face to face with an unintended result of our "good" work. Upon further investigation I found that some 1000 people a week were moving from the countryside to live on the sidewalks of Mumbai. They lost their homes, their livelihood, their way of life and even their social-religious structure. They were the street people and the new poor of India.

I was so moved that I said: "I want to give something for you to use for your children. Here is fifty dollars." She said: "Oh no, sir, that is too much. I cannot take that. She took twenty and pushed the rest back into my hand. As I walked back toward the hotel, I felt a tiny hand on my trousers tugging my pants leg. It was that little girl. She smiled at me and handed me a fresh cut flower.

Those people stayed in my memory and three years later I returned to Mumbai. My wife and I walked out on the sidewalk and not far from the IMC Chamber building across from the train station I saw her. She was there, but now her little girls had grown some. They were selling flowers woven into a little garland to people rushing to and from the train station. As I walked to Purnima she recognized me and smiled and said: "Oh sir, it is you. It has been a long time!" I asked her how she was doing. She said: "My husband was killed by a car one night as he was selling flowers. My oldest daughter suffers with an eye disease, but I work every day and pray that she can go to school some day. But kind sir, we are fine. "How are you?" "Fine" I said. I want to give you a gift." I started to hand her a twenty dollar bill and she said: "Oh no, sir. You were kind to us once and now you are a friend. I won't take your money." She let me buy some flowers from her little girls but she wouldn't accept a donation.

It was obvious to me that she was trapped on the streets of Mumbai. She would live and die there on the sidewalk. The odds are that her children will live a similar life because they don't have the resources or opportunity to escape.

The Bible says that the "poor are with you always." I know that is true and that we can't solve all of the problems of the world. But Purnima's problem might have been solved years earlier had people considered some things.

Did they consider the social impact and the social cost to building a dam and flooding out thousands of farmers? Did they consider the housing shortage in India and the implications of how to house and re-train the farmers who were affected? Could they have set up a structure in the cities to provide job placement, training and social services for these families? Could they have established an educational system to take the children of poor street- people to school, feed and cloth them and give them the educational tools to escape the prison of poverty? Was the consideration and value of the extra electricity produced from that power plant equal to the additional costs and losses thrust upon the people and the society?

The story of Purnima is a conundrum. It is the type of intellectual challenge that we must face and deal with in a better way. When I see a street person in any city on earth, whether it be on the mall of Washington D.C., or the underground sewers of Mongolia, I think of the millions of people like Purnima. They are trapped in their life style. Some become so accustomed to it that they don't want to live in any other way.

I was in Nepal being guided by two young street children. I had bought their breakfast and was pondering what would happen to these children. A German lady who had lived in Nepal told me that she had tried to deal with the same issues to the point of adopting street children. "You know, they would stay with me for a while but after going to school and enjoying clean clothes, and even the attraction of all the food they could want, they would still leave. They preferred the freedom of the streets to the structure of education. You have to get them very young to really change their lives."

I believe that she is right. The most effective way to deal with street poverty is to deal with the underlying causes for the poverty first. The next step is to attempt to redeem the children through good schooling and social support at an early age so as to break the "poverty cycle".

The conundrum of the poor and the story of Purnima

145

are offered as an encouragement to dedicate a portion of your intellect to dealing with their problems. They are in every city on earth. They are the product of poor leadership and poor policy. Yes the poor may be with us always, but we can't afford the luxury of allowing that to be an excuse to do nothing.

CHAPTER THIRTEEN

WRITING IN THE SAND, INITIALS IN THE SNOW

What is the significance of our lives? Sometimes metaphor is the connection between logic and reality, it "brings it across".

When I was a child, a few times we had the pleasure of driving all the way to the ocean for a holiday. I can remember those days on the beaches of Galveston Island, building sand forts, sand buildings, and creating multiple concentric walls to "defend" the fort against the relentless onslaught of the ocean. It was a great way to spend a day. Sometimes my mother or father helped, and using buckets we built towers in the sand. Sometimes we wrote messages in the Sand: "This is the beach of Ben Boothe...beware" only to see the foamy ocean wash it away.

It was revealing to get up the next morning, and see the spot of our fort, only as a slightly lower place on the beach...all of our "improvements" gone. It was the same when we went to the mountains in the winter. There we built snowmen, and wrote our initials in the snow...only to see them melt away. Are all the workings, the houses we build, the buildings, the businesses, the books we write, the poems we quote...are all of these just "writing in the sand" or "initials in the snow". Does it all simply melt away with the power and enormity of the universe?

Yes...and...No.

The things that we create sometimes extend the time that our "initials" stay. Look at the Taj Mahal, the Eiffel Tower, and the Empire State Building. Those are someone's sand castles and they still last. Look again at the twin towers of the World Trade Center or Pompey, or the arena/coliseum in Ancient Rome. They have melted away.

Some things last longer than others. Sometimes a poem, a love story, a book, a compelling idea, will last for thousands of years. Look at Socrates, Plato, Aristotle, Buddha, Christ, Moses, Abraham, Mohammed. They had a way of writing their initials into the hearts and minds of human thought and existence. Their initials have not melted away.

What about the love of a mother for her child. Does it melt away? Is it washed aside by the onslaught of the tide of busy existence?

There is a popular TV commercial. A young woman smiles at a man, he in turn helps open the door for an old person, the old person gives a contribution to a poor person, and it goes on. The love, the compassion of the person who started the "love" event, is multiplied and repeated and has an impact. Thus, could it be that the love and goodness of a Christ or a Buddha, has multiplied thousands of times. Could it be that the love that their mothers or fathers gave them is still replicating and blessing our lives?

Could it be that writing in the sand, or in the snow...could be permanent...as permanent as an idea?

When we send a telegraph, or make a telephone call, or send a fax, or send an e-mail...we are sending an electronic impulse that is so temporary that it goes away with lightening speed. It is more impermanent than the sand castle... Yet, the information, especially if impregnated with love, can be profoundly lasting...it can change lives...it can impact the world...

Thus, the proposition becomes...yes we can make initials in the sand, and if the right concept is powerful enough, perhaps it can become like sandstone. Or, yes, if the right environment of ideas is there, even an initial in the snow can become as hard as a glacier.

How do we make the products of our energies and our lives lasting?

We give them intellectual power. We give them love. We give them compassion. We try to see that we build things, and provide institutions and books that are filled with concepts showing that only divine blessing can be the ultimate origin.

Note what some have said about the significance and purpose in life.

WHY ARE WE HERE? WHAT IS THE PURPOSE OF IT ALL? Well, let's take a look at what some historic religions and individuals have said about this.

KRISHNA: Mike Robinson of the London Broadcasting Company asked Srila Prabhupada "Why do we exist in the first place?" The answer "The meaning of life is to enjoy. But now you are on a false platform of life and therefore you are suffering...but if you come to the real spiritual platform of life, then you'll enjoy." **The Science of Realization** by Srila Prabhupada

BUDDHISM: "Every human has an innate desire for happiness and does not want to suffer. The very purpose of life is to experience this happiness…to achieve it we must develop an ethical discipline and have compassion." Dalai Lama **An Open Heart-Practicing Compassion**

JUDAISM: "Fear God and keep his commandments, for this is the whole duty of man" Solomon Ecclesiastes 12:13

CHRISTIANITY: "You are the light of the world…let your light so shine before men that they may see your good works, and glorify your father" Jesus Christ Matt. 5:14 AND "there is faith, hope, and love, but the greatest of these is love." Apostle Paul I Cor 13

PLATO: "The goal of humanity is to find happiness"

ATHEIST: "Happiness and pleasure instead of sorrow and pain" stated Howard Holmes in a letter on Atheism. A common idea mentioned again and again is the concept that to find happiness, we should seek to do "good", motivated by love and compassion. But the key is not just to "Do" but to "Be".

CHAPTER FOURTEEN

ॐ ✡ ☿ ☾★ ✵ 🧘 ॐ ∞ ☯ ✝

SECULAR VS RELIGIOUS IS NOT THE QUESTION

Tsagaach Geleg was born in Mongolia while it was under Russian influence in 1973. Her father was a school teacher and witnessed the fifty year reign of Russia. Mongolia had been a Buddhist nation for over 500 years until the Communist party took over leadership of the government. By the time Mongolia declared independence in 1990, nearly all of the temples and monasteries had been destroyed and thousands of Buddhist monks imprisoned or executed.

Tsagaach Geleg was raised in a traditional Buddhist family but went through the University of Mongolia under a Communist philosophy. Like many of her generation, she received conflicting signals about religion and society. The Communist system taught a secular system. But then she was approved to go the United States for advanced education. While at Texas Christian University, her perspective deepened and broadened until at the age of 30 she told me: "Now I can go to the Buddhist temple with my parents and pray and feel uplifted and inspired. But I can also go to a Christian church and worship and feel uplifted and inspired. But even if there is no temple or church available, even in a secular society like the one Russia imposed on Mongolia, I pray often knowing that my prayers are heard."

It is remarkable that in the most difficult and challenging of circumstances Tsagaach has become a good and spiritual individual. It is thrilling that she does not feel the need to condemn or exclude those of different religious traditions. She can participate and benefit from a Buddhist culture, a Christian culture and even can experience prayer life in a secular culture. She reflects the connected global generation.

Some intellectuals question as to whether cultures should be secular or religious. It is a life or death battle in Islamic nations. But even the West struggles with the question. In 2003 leaders of the European Union met in Greece to vote on a constitution to govern 450 million Europeans. The most controversial debate was whether to acknowledge Christianity's impact on European culture! Europe has evolved into a secular society but many forces want to deny the historical Christian influence. The Christian Pope argues that Christianity must be highlighted, while Western Europe's 15 million Muslims oppose it.

The question as to whether a nation should be religious or secular is not relevant when considering the emerging religion of the global generation. Many people view contrasting systems but the very manner of defining the contrasts suggests conflict. For example, the fundamentalist Islamic cleric thinks that his culture, government, and society must be absolutely religious. The British citizen thinks that his culture, government and society must be absolutely secular. The typical American believes that his society is religious but wants to keep government secular.

In truth, the British pro-Western society and culture is

not absolutely secular. There are thousands of shades of secularism and religion in the secular culture. Everything from architecture, legal systems, cultural norms, and ethical values, has a basis in the various religious influences that have been a part of Western history. The opposite is true in fundamentalist Islamic nations. The culture, nation, and society in Pakistan, for example, are not absolutely religious! Look at the food, clothing, or music. Even traditional fundamentalist countries have secular influences. The current aggressive definitions tend to increase judgementalism and tend to extend popular myths about society. All of us are religious. All of us are secular. Indeed the new global religion recognizes this. We do not have to align ourselves with one sect or another. But we *can at the same time continue to love, appreciate and be a part of the religious heritage that we feel the most comfortable with.* On an individual basis, we recognize within our own religious experience that the religious tradition that we were raised in is not totally consistent either. It is not totally religious and not totally secular; elements of both will be in any system of thought.

Therefore it is easier to not be judgmental or divisive. It is easier to see the common aspects, the ethics of love, acceptance, respect, honor, and fairness, and to see that they are pervasive in any idealistic human ideology. Why judge or destroy another individual who holds within himself some of the same beautiful aspirations of existence that you hold? We all fear pain, punishment and death. If we share the common fears, understand common pain, then why would we ever consider inflicting pain, punishment and death upon others? Because in doing so, we are inflicting the same upon ourselves. We are one.

When the Challenger disintegrated above our heads in Texas, Saturday, February 1, 2003, we actually witnessed the moment of the death of those Astronauts. We looked into the sky to see a beautiful, almost breathtaking point of light with the magnificent vapor contrail. Then, it divided into two, then four, then eight, and then a veritable fireworks display of pieces and particles falling through the sky. All who saw it knew that death and destruction, "the moment", the instant of death and destruction was implanted into our consciousness. The entire world felt the common sadness and knowledge of witnessing the death of those astronauts. In our imaginations, we all wondered about those last instants of life and the transition to death. In doing so, we participated in the fact that we are all one. We were one with them; because we dramatically saw the instant…we imagined their fear, horror, and death. We wondered what the sudden transition to death must have been like for them…we were there with them in our minds. On that morning, at 8:03 A.M.Central Standard Time, I was at my Boothe Ranch. I walked to the Stupa gazed at the cool winter blue sky; the sunshine was beautiful. The birds were singing and flitting through the trees of the prayer garden, and a squirrel was hopping through the tree limbs. I felt such a deep peace at that moment. I knew, in that moment, that those Astronauts had already made their transition to a greater existence within the whole. I knew that they were in peace. They were past the pain, the work, the terror…they were at one with the heavens and the earth. They were at one with all of us. They were at peace. But, in truth, they always were, at one with the heavens and with all of us, but their lives, egos, existence as astronauts just distracted them from the realization of the ultimate fact. We were the ones in pain because we had not processed all of the information

154

yet. Peace would come to our hearts when we - in reflection - realized that we were also a part of the whole. A poet created a lyric that suggested that these astronauts "sought the heavens and abide there". I might suggest that we all "seek the heavens, and abide in the heaven of each other".

We are one. Whatever our religious, secular or sectarian heritage, we should be at peace. Peace is a part of the journey to enlightened thought.

CHAPTER FIFTEEN

ॐ ✡ ☿ ☪ ✺ 🧘 ॐ ∞ ☯ ✝

A LITTLE SALT CAN SEASON THE ENTIRE WORLD

What impact can a well-focused group have on the world at large? In India, the Jain religion is a strict, ancient religion, similar in many respects to Buddhism, except that the intellectual and religious standards are stricter. Jains have managed to keep their intellectual growth alive through the century, and have a deep-set reverence for the sanctity of life. They do not kill. They even screen the earth, to remove earthworms before they farm it, so as not to kill even a tiny worm. They are vegetarians, and they have a strong alliance to their traditions and temples. In south India, Jains have become the doctors, lawyers, and intellectuals. They control great wealth, because they have been organized, educated, and at peace for generations. They have a great impact, far beyond their numbers, in India, and the region. They create prosperity, and an intellectual leavening for the social culture in the region.

Another example is the "Davos Group". Every year about 1000 businessmen, bankers, government officials, intellectuals and journalists gather at the World Economic Forum in Davos, Switzerland. These are well-educated people. The "Davos Group" is very powerful. They control, or have great influence upon the vast majority of international institutions, many of the world's governments, and the majority of the economic and military powers of the world.

Buddhism is the only major world religion that does not have a corresponding world power nation/ civilization. I believe the reason is that Buddhism, unlike every other major world religion, did not force its philosophy upon a nation by military force. Islam, Judaism, and Christianity, all created "political/ military" forces and therefore nation-states emerged. But Buddhism simply migrated from Nepal, to India, then to China, then throughout the region. One of the central tenants of the religion is non-violence, peace, and compassion to others. Thus, in a very real sense, here is a thought philosophy that has permeated a culture of millions of people, without dominating them by military or political force.

By these three examples, and there could be many more, we can see that a well focused, well educated group can have enormous influence and impact upon the world at large. The new religion of the global generation is destined to be like these examples. The thinking, the intellect, the moral force, the spiritual energy, can have a powerful impact upon the world at large. Like the Jains of India, or the "Davos Group", the group will be like a global salt that "seasons" the intellectual, spiritual, political, and cultural world at large. Why is this?

The fact is that ALL OF HUMANITY IS RELATED. Even with varied cultures and many different civilizations, we all come from one root. We are brothers and sisters. In spite of the different geography, religion, and cultures that represent the vast ocean of our differences, there exists a vast river of commonality. For example, moral values, such as "thou shalt not steal" "thou shall not lie" "thou shalt not cheat thy fellow man" "You will show compassion to others" "kindness and generosity are virtues"... these types of values, can, if we will let them, unite all of mankind. The common humanity of love, sex, mystery, heroism, sacrifice, self-improvement, these are something we all share. Plus global communications continue to bring us together, joining mutual images, ideas, and experiences. We have learned that different languages are not insurmountable obstacles to human relations. In terms of religious symbols, the more humans interact, the more that we learn about the religion and cultures of others. We have found common, archetypal symbols representing deity, good, power, love, energy, sexual power, compassion, that seem to emerge in every religion. While the symbols may differ with the geography or religion, the basic meanings and impulses are common to all humanity.

Increased trade, investment, tourism, media, and communication tends to help us recognize that we do have commonality with all mankind. Urbanization, increasing literacy, increasing education, affluence, and the tremendous expansion of scientific and engineering knowledge have increased our understanding of the value of traditional cultures, plus the value of modern cultures. The children of the global generation will understand and develop systems that cherish both traditional values while allowing enjoyment of modern cultures. One of the major forces of violence in the world today is the fear and anxiety of those who believe and want to live by "ancient traditional culture" and their fear that modern culture will destroy the important values of their heritage. We will find avenues of solution and peace for these people.

There is a sign in Fort Worth, Texas, that simply states: "Where the West begins". This cowboy city promotes its proud tradition of historic western themes with rodeos, western music, western foods, clothing, and western social customs. At the rodeos, the city assures that there is a dose of traditional religious values taught ostensibly "for the children", but it is also a way of assuring the culture that there is respect for the traditional values. On the other hand, the city has modern and sophisticated technological developments including museums, educational institutions, and very progressive cultural pockets. Indeed the city has been able to preserve much of the value of the traditional culture and Christian religion, yet the community over all has a diverse society with Hindus, Islamic, Buddhist temples, and a general tolerance - even encouragement - of freedom and diversity.

This is what is needed in a global scope. The fundamentalist Muslim groups seem to be fighting for their traditions of the 7th century. They need to see a culture and society that will allow, even encourage their traditional beliefs, while still enjoying the advances of the modern age. The concept of tolerance and specific teaching on the concepts of tolerance for others is desperately needed, especially in areas of fundamental militarism. This type of teaching brings the concept of individual freedom and tolerance and respect for individuals. This implies that there will be separation of church and state. This concept, so well articulated by Thomas Jefferson, and Mahatma Gandhi, and Nehru, is central to a peaceful world. The Hindu civilizations of the past seem to have recognized this. In Islam, God is like a Caesar. In China and Japan, the nation's rulers are considered God. In Russia, God is like a junior partner to the government leadership. In the United States, and in the West in general, the separation of church and state has been central to the peaceful development of cultures and societies, and is also a major factor in the development of personal freedom, personal incentives, and the energetic personal power that one has when he knows he can try to achieve his personal aspirations, whether they be political, economic, or social.

In recent years, the concept of separation of church and state has been attacked by those who would try to make America and other nations, lands of intolerance, and in the process, destroy the concepts of brotherhood, multiculturalism and educated tolerance.

Don Woodard is a prominent businessman and author in Ft.Worth, Texas, and is a brilliant student of American history. He told me recently, "America is seeing a rampant McCarthyism; an intolerance for others and almost violent opposition to any person who has a different opinion". The same week, Joe Orr, an attorney who leads the World Affairs Council of Tarrant County and has spent his life encouraging foreigners to visit America and to encourage multi-cultural exchanges, indicated his alarm at the "McCarthy type attitudes that have emerged in America".

It is the children of the global generation , who will define, discuss, and bring these concepts to the fore, to create a better, more peaceful, more unified world. This group epitomizes the value and power of "multi-cultural" thought. Their ideas, concepts and practical applications will be incredibly influential throughout the world. It is not the number, but the quality, the intensity of the intellectual effort, plus the energy and integrity of this generation that is important. Those who are members of the new global religion, will have unparalleled influence in the future of the world. The children of the global generation can have, will have, and are having an influence for peace in the world, and this trend has the potential to grow exponentially.

CHAPTER SIXTEEN

☦ ✡ ♇ ☪ ❖ 🧘 ॐ ⸒ ☯ ✝

LOVE AND RELATIONSHIPS

Where does love fit in the religion of the new global generation ?

It is central. It is the foundation, the peak, it is everything. The religion of the global generation has the central ethic that people matter. People are to be loved. This requires that we do away with barriers to relationships. This requires love and a commitment not to hurt others and to treat all with compassion. From the most primitive tribal group to the most sophisticated social clicks in Paris, walls, inhibitors and codes have been developed to stop relationships. Our outlook on life in the world is that people throughout the globe are all related. We are brothers and sisters who ultimately come from the same stock. We then must learn to communicate or relate in spite of barriers that history and culture have artificially created. Why do we keep placing barriers to block the command "Love one Another"?

I saw a young woman in an airport recently. She was an image of fear and discomfort. She walked through the lobby fearfully clutching her things. I could see the fear and protective body language that she shielded up and it made me sad. I wanted to walk up to her and say: "It's ok. We are all facing the same obstacles of transportation and connections. We are all trying to cope with additional security, the weight and discomfort of luggage, and 99% of the people here are just like you. It's ok, let me help you."

Sometimes we are able to make contact in spite of the social barriers. I've noticed that people who travel more seem more secure in life's experiences and tend to take down barriers easier. It is basic in life. My mother, while in her seventies, once told me: "Ben, love is rare and beautiful in life. You should cherish it because some people live their lives in misery, quenching it and making other people miserable. Those who receive and give love have so much more happiness. Take all the happiness that you can."

It is all about relationships. Are we willing to open up to relationships? Think of cloistered people controlled by religious clerics or social constraints that don't even allow them to speak to another person, or who cannot read or go to school? Their ability to "love their fellow man" is restricted by angry men who foster the power to control others. Is there something evil about a brotherhood and sisterhood of mankind? Is there something wrong with letting love and communication and compassion flourish? No, it is just that when love flourishes it tends to destroy barriers and the artificial social walls that institutions, culture, society, churches, politics and even businesses have developed.

In your work, and your travels around your neighborhood or around the world, make it your life quest to break down barriers. If you find yourself on an airplane or in a crowded place, try to study the faces of people and observe the 'hard cases' so as to figure ways to break the barriers. The results are often astonishing. Some of your good friends around the world might be introduced to you in this way. I recall a woman in the first class section of an airplane who seemed to bring a dark cloud of sorrow in the airplane with her. Finally, we were able to visit, to laugh, and to share. A month later I got a letter from her. She explained that she had just lost a son to AIDS, and was considering suicide. She said: "I didn't want to talk to anyone but your kind nature prodded me to a conversation. I don't know why or how, but you saved my life and gave me hope to live again." Of course if I blessed her, her letter blessed me many times in return.

I was running late to make a connection for an international flight in Los Angeles. As I ran up to the counter they announced a limit of one carry-on bag. I was frustrated because I had two bags with valuables in them. Then I heard a kind voice coming from a young lady from Costa Rica say: "That's ok. I'll carry your extra bag for you. I will fight for you if they give trouble." It was a joyful gift of kindness that she spontaneously gave. What is that kind of behavior? In essence, it is pure love.

The effort, the allowance to go forth in life willing to remove or break through barriers and offer "love" is a gift to all mankind. It is one of the central gifts of the citizens of the global generation. Why? Because love is central. It is the foundation, it is the core, it is the circle, and it is the reason. Without it, the human soul cannot truly grow. The churches and religions that have lost their growth and vitality have, in fact, lost their love. It has been replaced by institutional rules and traditions. Their vigor has drifted away. Our vigor is the vigor of love. It creates tension, energy, joy, happiness. It is the source and the result of our belief in nirvana, God, heaven, and enlightenment.

CHAPTER SEVENTEEN

ॐ ✡ ☥ ☪ ❖ 🧘 ॐ ∞ ☯ ✝

PARADOX OF TIME
AND SPACE

We have considered the paradox of time. Time is this entity, this idea created by man, that there is a way to measure the eternal. We understand the concept that time is finite. The idea that it is unchangeable is not true. Einstein taught us that time is relative, that if you are traveling at the speed of light, that time slows down, and that ultimately space bends. We know that something about time in our own experience is relative. For in moments of intensity, time seems to go slow. In times of laxity, time seems to "zip by". A young person says that it will take forever for him to grow up. An old person looks back and speaks of how quickly it all passed. Time, thus is relative. Not a fixed dot on a clock. Yet in our world of business and schedules and our "new" reality, we make time into something like a judge, god, and standard that we must all abide by.

Space may also be relative. I think of the people who go into meditation. They soon find that the smallest room or the smallest cave can become comfortable and enormous as they explore the wonders of their mind. We know that as children our homes seemed so large because they were filled with our experiences and discovery. Then when we go back a few years later, our childhood homes have become smaller. Our world has enlarged, our experiences spread out, and the space of that home seems smaller. But if we were to re-enter that home, and make it the center and focus of our existence, it would expand and grow again.

It is much the same with a commercial building, a church, a city, or a state...even the world. As our focus and experience intensifies and focuses, we find that the world, a state, a city, or a church can grow...or shrink. Space is also a relative term when placed in perspective of the human experience.

The world seems to become more compact if we fly over it in a jet airplane. It is less compact if we are in a ship. The world grows larger if we cross the ocean in a life raft, or cross a desert on a bicycle or horse.

The world of Jesus was very small...a tiny country, and travel was by foot, or by mule. Yet His tiny country seems like an empire when one reads of the life of Jesus, with all of the experiences and intensity His life reflected. Buddha lived most of his life in what is known as Northern India, primarily between Bod Gaya, Sarnath, India, and Lumbini in Nepal. It was a relatively small area. Yet a review of his life seems to encompass a large world. His space was expanded. Indeed his time was expanded, as was that of Jesus, for they continue to live in the lives of others.

So, this thing called time is no doubt hard to understand, except that to say that to know time is to know eternity, and to know now is to know eternity, and to know here, this place, here and now is to know the entire globe in an eternal sense.

Thus the person who can say: "I am" is blessed with

insight. The person who can say: "This is now…this is my moment" has an insight. The person who can say: "I am here fully" has deep insight. The person who can say: "I am here and now" has enormous insight. That person may understand the divine element of self perception. To have all of these understandings, without an element of negative ego…is all the more powerful. Meditate on these:

I am.

I touch eternity by touching now.

I am here.

I am, here and now.

Wow.

Breathe in.

Breathe out.

I am.

This is now.

Breathe in.

I am here.

Breathe out.

I am here and now

I am alive!

I am awake!

Smile.

CHAPTER EIGHTEEN

ॐ ✡ ♆ ☾ ❖ 🧘 ॐ ∞ ☯ ✝

WHERE HAVE ALL THE PROPHETS GONE?

Prophets. Think of them. What are they like? How does society respond to them? The question is in order because the Children of the global generation, by nature will be prophets. Prophets are not usually popular people. History tells us that those who have a prophetic voice generally get under the skin of society in general. We, as a rule are made uncomfortable by prophets. But, prophets have a vision of things that they are compelled to share. Prophets are typically on the "leading edge" of thinking, and that tends to make people nervous. Prophets, such as those in the Old Testament of the Bible did outrageous things, such as growing their hair long, fasting for months and sometimes years, and going to great extremes, sometimes almost over dramatic, to get their message across. The Prophets of other cultures have similar characteristics. A few years ago, I asked a prominent attorney, John Allen Chalk, to speak to a group on the subject of: WHERE HAVE ALL THE PROPHETS GONE? John Allen Chalk is a man at home both in his law office of Texas or in the company of Prime Ministers as he travels the world. When I asked him what happened to the visionary prophets he said: "They are gone! People tend to destroy prophets. They are often too threatening!"

Prophets, in modern vernacular, are on the leading edge of thinking, culture, philosophy, ethics and morality.

168

They are sometimes avid defenders of the ethical core of traditional values, but not necessarily institutional or political precepts. Consider the prophets of the biblical Old Testament such as Jeremiah, Ezekiel, Hezekiah, Isaiah, and others. They were outrageous non-conformists. Look at some of their traits: Courageous. Colorful. Willing to do unusual things to get their message across. Prophets are, above all, richly committed to the message. They feel that their message is not only theirs, but more importantly, it is the word of God! Consider the prophets of Islam. Colorful. Unique. Creative. Filled with energy and mystique. Consider the prophets of Tibet. The 12th Dalai Lama, and the 13th, both accurately prophesied historical events. The 13th Dalai Lama, just a few years before his death predicted the Chinese invasion with "They will rape our women, kill our monks, burn our Temples and try to destroy our culture". The 14th Dalai Lama saw a similar vision shortly before 1947, just before China overran the country.

But generally, prophets have not been well accepted by mainstream society. Acceptance requires a mature, sensitive, insightful and tolerant culture to appreciate and understand. A great thinker said: "Prophetic ideas at first exposure are ridiculed. Then the ideas are feared, and opposed. Then, the ideas are accepted as the truth." Sometimes prophets are so unorthodox and non-conformist that they make rank and file cultures uncomfortable. But, part of their job is to take people out of their comfort zones, to challenge them, to require them to think, to force people to stretch. Their role is to force people to think. Sometimes the process of thinking creates conflict...inner, outer, worldly, spiritual, ethical, etc.

Sometimes prophets communicate the "words of God, or words of Truth". It is just that most people in the conformist main stream cannot see all of God or all of truth. But at least they see aspects of God and truth with clarity. Anyone, such as a prophet, who sees more, or sees well, will tend to challenge all who hear them. Like a mirror light disco-ball that hangs in a ballroom with hundreds of mirrors that reflect and shine throughout the room, we can see the bright reflection of perhaps one, or two, or a dozen of the mirrors, but we cannot see them all. We don't have that capacity. A person might see a bright light as it pans across his face which is just a fraction of the whole. But most people can't grasp or get their minds around all of the hundreds of light rays that are flowing in different directions in the room.

A prophet often has the capacity to see, to stand back and see the overall impact of what is going on in the room...he sees from many different perspectives. The prophet can see how the hundreds of lights are impacting the crowd. He can see the overall impact of the room. He has something to communicate because he observes more. He takes time to think about what he observes. He has the "presence" to "be there". He doesn't just wait until the one light reflects upon his eye...he sees more...he sees many...he sees a bigger picture. He sees the impact that the light was hung on the ceiling for.

So where have all of the prophets gone? Basic to the nature of a prophet is that he doesn't have to agree with people. He doesn't have to be popular. Neither his point of view nor his concept of the core truths that he sees is important. He doesn't require popularity. He requires that people understand what is going on below the surface. Truth sometimes makes people feel uncomfortable.

So where have prophets in OUR time gone? Where are OUR Jeremiahs, or Ezekiel's? Where are OUR prophets? The question is critical, because history teaches that prophets often make people so uncomfortable that society tends to drive away prophets unless it is an enlightened, compassionate, or tolerant society.

Where are the prophets? They are often driven away! No one wants to have his or her security shell cracked or challenged. Thus, as Children of the global generation evolve into prophets, they will find that often they threaten others...because they are causing them the discomfort of thinking, and thinking often leads to the collision of conflicting ideas, ideas that must conflict to bring out the core values, and then to find core truth and social responsibility.

Claire Villereal graduated from one of the best universities in America, Rice University. Then she went on a trip to Tibet to observe and learn. She told me this story from India about the threatening nature of truth.

'A king was pre-warned by his wise men, that a poison rain would fall and cause mental illness. He put out a proclamation to his people warning them not to drink the rain water, but as the rain fell into the creeks and lakes, people drank it anyway. They became crazy. After a while, everyone in his kingdom was crazy. Then they began to attack and criticize the king, because he was different. They accused him of all kinds

171

of things, and became more and more violent. Soon, all of the mentally ill people of his kingdom decided that the king was crazy, and threatened to kill him if he didn't drink the water. He couldn't bear the pressure. He was the only sane one left, and the entire world around him was crazy, but it was too hard for him. Finally, he drank the water.'

Prophets in a culture are often subjected to that kind of pressure. It takes courage and strength to be a prophet.

But there is another rule. As surely as prophets are driven out, they reappear. They reappear because the moral imperative of life requires someone to "see" for society, and to help define things, to help people understand what they see. Society needs people of perspective, people who haven't drunk the "polluted waters" of ignorance. People. Societies. Cultures. Civilizations need prophets. So...they appear. They come to the world scene when they are needed. They are called.

Who are they? Where do they come from? We (I'm speaking of you and I, reader) may be destined by the fact that we have shared this dialogue this far, to make others uncomfortable. It may be inevitable – especially as you share these multi-cultural and multi-spiritual ideas with other. If we observe, think, research, analyze, probe, challenge, inquire, nudge, and see the inconsistencies and the untruths that powerful political and institutional manipulators of this world thrust upon the naïve public...you and I are destined to be prophets. Because this time, this era, calls for prophets. History shows that prophets come, they are "called" by some invisible force when mankind needs them. Our world needs prophets now, more than ever. We may become prophets if we can see the entire ballroom; if we can see the overall impact of the light as it is reflected, refracted, and bounced into the eyes of people, and if we can see the impact that the brief touch of light has on them, and if we can see the impact of the whole. If you can see these things, if you can get your mind around the nature of truth, and the source, and the impact, and the question of why, then you are destined to be a prophet of this time. You have been called.

THINK WELL.

THINK HONESTLY

THINK ONLY OF GOOD WILL.

THINK REALITY.

THINK WITH COMPASSION.

THINK WITH GRACE.

and then,

SPEAK WELL.

SPEAK HONESTLY.

SPEAK WITH GOOD WILL.

SPEAK REALITY.

SPEAK WITH COMPASSION.

SPEAK WITH GRACE.

...the grace to do as the Dalai Lama has done so well.
LIVE WITH HUMILITY AND WITH A QUICK SMILE
AND GOOD WIT.

I look forward to

KNOWING YOUR RESULTS,

SEEING YOUR COMPASSION, AND,

ENJOYING YOUR SMILE.

MAKE A DIFFERENCE.

It is your divine opportunity.

CHAPTER-NINETEEN

ॐ ✡ ☿ ☾✦ ❀ 🧘 ॐ ∞ ☯ ✝

ACTION AND PARALYSIS

"I don't know what to do, or how to help!" said a man during a business luncheon in March of 2003. The polls had come out. 47% of Americans were against a war in Iraq. 43% were for a war. This man was in the group that opposed the war. He said: "I just feel bad about our country. I feel bad about the direction our nation is going. We are fighting a war, ruining the economy, and it seems that as citizens, we are helpless to stop it or do anything about it." Millions of Americans felt the same way. But, if further investigation were made, probably, most people who opposed the war had done nothing. Those who wanted war were well organized and determined to proceed.

This was the same response that the citizens of Germany took in the 1930's when their government was being taken over and led in violent and warlike directions by Hitler and his cronies. It was a response of doing nothing while feeling helpless in the face of bad leadership. Inevitably, when good, well informed people do nothing, bad people will fill the gap with action.

INERTIA. Some have negative inertia, some with positive inertia. The inertia of doing nothing is powerful. Excuses for inertia are almost like a mantra: "I am too old, too tired, too young, too poor, too educated, too ignorant, too well known, not well known enough, too busy, too much obligated to an institution or a group,

175

too obligated to an image, too sick, too weak, too polite, too controlled by inertia.". Most of us paralyze ourselves.

But, life for us, the "global generation" demands that we be a friend to mankind. Our social imperative is that we be humanists; that we love humanity. It requires that we understand how important it is to be a friend to others. It has been said that a friend walks into your life when everyone else is walking out. In 1999 Gary Gardner was such a friend to a group of Negro young people. Gary lived in Vigo Park, Texas, which was a small village of one store, a small shop, a church and five houses. Nearby in the town of Tulia, forty six teenagers had just been indicted on drug charges. "There is something wrong about it" Gary told me. "First of all, I personally know some of these kids and they are good kids. Secondly, it is an odd coincidence that nearly all of them are black kids." he said. Gary investigated further and made a decision to challenge the court, the Sheriff's office and the establishment of Tulia. On December 28, 1999 he wrote a letter to the editor of the local newspaper standing up for those kids. By the words of that letter, he blew the whistle on a great injustice. Some in Tulia were furious that he made a public issue of it. Gary received irate and threatening calls. But Gary continued to press for an investigation. He became involved in trying to broaden exposure of the issue statewide and wanted to take the friends and relatives of the imprisoned kids to the capital of the state; Austin, Texas. But Gary had a problem since he didn't have the money to pay for chartering a bus, so he met with his family and reviewed their farm income. They had government CRP payments... the precious income from his farmland that they had planned to use to put in the next year's crop. But, they made the decision to use it for the bus expense. "We felt that participation in those trips was important for the kids who had been put in jail," he said.

The national press became involved as investigations found that many of these kids had been indicted, convicted and imprisoned on false information planted by a racist undercover agent. On June 16, 2003, twelve of the thirty eight kids that had been convicted were released by the courts and Gary Gardner proudly stood by them as they walked out of the Swisher County Court House.

Gary Gardner didn't have to act. It would have been easier for him to do nothing. But he was willing to act. If you ever visit Vigo Park, Texas, you should look Gary Gardner up. He will probably be wearing the same hat he has worn for over twenty years; a large brimmed western felt hat with a hole in the top. He will have on coveralls and old boots. But he is an excellent model for the global generation, because he cares enough to act in face of ignorance and injustice. In this world sometimes attacks on humanity are intellectual, sometimes ethical, and sometimes attacks of evil conflict. This is the time that good people should "walk in" and give others the benefit of their intellect and energy.

Be a friend.

You are significant and important, and it is important that you communicate to others, and to the world, that they too are significant, and important, and that you know the difficulty that humanity faces. We cannot allow ignorance, bigotry, greed, warmongering, power mongering, cruelty, murder, divisiveness and fear dominate our world. We will not, you and me. This is

God-work (good work) that we are engaged in; work that is more important than ourselves. This work will impact your children and grandchildren and the children of mothers in far away lands.

You understand.

You are thinking about those who are suffering.

You will be there for them, if they need you.

You are willing to help to the extent of your abilities.

Your mind, your voice, your pen, your brush, your energy and spirit, your compassion are called.

THIS IS YOUR TIME TO ACT.

The famous black baseball hero, Satchel Page, once said: "Just hit the balls that are thrown to you." Life can throw us many curves and all that we can do is deal with what comes our way. But, if we do not swing, we can't hit anything! We must act within the framework of our lives.

What do you see in the world that is causing it to be dominated by ignorance or shallow thinking?

Where can you contribute?

To whom can you offer words of insight and give them the courage to move forward to another level?

Where can you challenge and turn the light into the dark corners of ignorance?

Where can you show compassion?

You are not alone. We, fellow flowers facing the sun are there with you and look forward to meeting you on the journey.

Reader, I've enjoyed sharing this moment in the universe together.

CHAPTER TWENTY

☮ ✡ ☿ ☪ ❈ 🧘 ॐ ⳾ ☯ ✝

THOUGHTS TO PONDER IN A QUIET MOMENT

One does not speak with kind words to become kind…
A kind person is compelled to act in kind ways.

One does not do compassionate things to become a
compassionate person…A person who is compassionate
is compelled to act in compassionate ways.

One does not do good things to become a good
person…A good person just does good things.

One does not act in humble ways to become humble…
A humble person simply cannot be otherwise.

One does not do "generous" things to become
generous…A generous heart radiates generosity in all
that the person does.

We cannot be except what we are. The further you go
away from your center, the more inner conflict you have.
Remember the words that God used for his name: "I
Am". I am is the most central foundation thought of
every person's existence. I Am. I can tell you that "You
Are" love, and there is God within you. The greeting of
India, Namaste' means, "I bless the God in you". Or "I
bless the Buddha in you" Or "I bless the light in you."

At the critical junction of all human relationships there

is a key point, a key question, THE question:

What would love do now?

If we accept the premise that we are all part of one whole, then what you do to others, you do to yourself for **there is no other**.

Therefore, bless all relationships.

Your personal relationships are holy ground.

You must first honor, cherish, and love yourself.

See the good in you.

See the God in you.

See the Buddha, the Krishna and Shiva in you.

You are not fear, you are love. When you experience that love, then you can see the good in others, honor them, cherish them, and love them.
The highest thought is that which brings Joy.

The clearest word, the clearest understanding, is Truth.

The greatest feeling is Love.

Love, Truth and Joy. One always leads to another. It doesn't matter which order they are placed in. Spin them, mix them up and watch how they point to one another.

Namaste'

ॐ ✡ ☿ ☪ ✤ 🧘 卐 ∞ ☯ ✝

EPILOGUE:
COMPASSION, A VIEW FROM
WEST TEXAS

My Grandfather was a Texas farmer and rancher in the 1930's, 40's, and 50's. One year his farms produced bumper crops, and after that Grandfather Middleton was considered almost a gentleman farmer. After that good year, he always drove a Cadillac and every day he made it out to the country to check the crops and talk to his farmers. He was a distinctive man and always wore a conservative grey western suit, Stetson "25" hat, and dress western boots.

Merchants, businessmen, and even bankers knew that his word was his bond. When a neighbor's farm equipment broke down, grandfather would show up to bring their crops in for them. When families in the area needed a doctor or couldn't afford groceries "Papau" as we called him, took care of them.

My grandfather died in 1953 and yet his name still has brightness about it in West Texas. My mother is now in her seventies and in 2002 she went to a high school reunion in O'Donnell, Texas. A woman came up to her and said: "Back in the late 1940's, your father drove by our house one day as us children were playing ball. We were poor, and only had a rounded rock and some old tree limbs and sticks to play with. He sat in his Cadillac and watched us a while and drove away, and later returned. We watched with surprise and joy as he quietly

182

got out of his car and set new baseball bats, balls, and gloves on the sidewalk... He never said a word, and quietly drove away. My family, brothers and sisters, all thought he was the greatest man...so full of dignity, charisma, power, and...compassion. I just wanted you to know that about your daddy."

A few years later, my grandfather was hospitalized for peptic ulcers and the doctors in Lamesa had poor equipment and scant knowledge on how to treat him. But he was losing a lot of blood and so they told my grandmother that the hospital was out of blood and they needed donors. The word went throughout Dawson County, that "Dewie Middleton was in trouble, he needed help now...could you give blood"? Within an hour, lines of people came "To help Mr. Middleton". So many people came that the hospital doctor said that he had never seen anything like it.

The doctors couldn't stop the bleeding, and he died. At the funeral hundreds of people the family didn't know showed up. People that he had given a boost to, children he had helped with school expenses, farmers that he had helped, families that he had paid hospital bills for. Many stories were told about my Papa that we had never known...and we learned that he impacted the lives of many.

He was a rough hewn, tough man, without a college degree. He had never traveled to India to the home of Buddha, or to Israel to learn the lessons of Moses, or Jesus. But he understood the concept of compassion and love. It was in him. It was his inner fire. He didn't do good things to "make points". He did them because he was compelled to...it was his "inner light". As I write this in 2003, his name still shines brightly across the plains of West Texas.

Isn't it noteworthy, that a man's reputation, his good will, his compassion would continue to shine, some 50 years after his death?

He was not a particularly religious man, at least not in public. He rarely went to church. But in some ways he exemplified a life of charity and compassion that the Church always sought from its most faithful members. He avoided church ritual, but if the church needed help or funds, he was always a generous patron. Perhaps he knew long before the "global generation" that regardless of our religious preferences, we are all "FLOWERS FACING THE SUN".

A WORD OF THANKS AND A PARTIAL BILIOGRAPHY

It has been said that no idea is unique. I am thankful to the many people, teachers, friends, scholars and authors who have shared ideas that may have surfaced in this small book. My perspective comes from a university degree in Theology, then a transition from that into the business world of Wall Street stock brokerage, to banking and finance. As a C.E.O. of several banks I began to see economic trends and question the loss of ethical foundations for financial policies that impacted the lives of people. The U.S.I.A. (State Department) and World Bank recruited me as a consultant with 'hands on experience in bank management' to teach those in developing nations how to put together banking systems and to restructure financial systems after times of crisis. One day it occurred to me. Financial systems are not for the benefit of money. They are for the benefit of people. Thereafter, as I circled the globe and observed socio-economic systems first hand, I saw things in a 'people' perspective. Every person I have met, every book I have read, every experience has in some way contributed to this book. Thus, there is no claim of that "unique" idea in this effort but there is a deep gratitude to all who have helped me along the way. The following books and authors are particularly cited with thanks for concepts that came out in different ways in this book and I recommend them to you. Thanks to all of you.

The Bible by various Hebrew and Christian authors over a 4000 year period.

The Clash of Civilizations and the Remaking of World Order by Robert Kaplan and Samuel Huntington, 2002

When Religion Becomes Evil by Charles Kimball 2003, Harper Collins Books

The Science of Self Realization by Bhaktivedama Swami Prabhupada 1977, Bhaktivedanta Book Trust

The Assassins (Radical Sect in Islam) by Bernard Lewis 1967 Basic Books

Going Home (Jesus Buddha as Brothers) by Thich Nhat Hanh Riverhead Books

Living Buddha, Living Christ by Thich Nhat Hanh Riverhead Books

How the Great Religions Began by Joseph Gaer 1929 Signet Key Books

The Hero with a Thousand Faces by Joseph Campbell 1968 Bollingen Series, Princeton University

Myths to Live By by Joseph Campbell 1972 Penguin Books

Secrets of the Vajra World by Reginald Ray 2002 Shambhala Books

Terror in the Mind of God by Mark Juergensmeyer 2000 University of California Press.

Beyond Belief by U.S. Naipaul 1998 Vintage Books

Disposable People by Kevin Bales 1999 University of California Press

The Himalayan Poverty Threat To The World by Krishna Bahadur Kunwar 2002 Meena Publication, Nepal

Encountering God: A Spritual Journey from Bozeman to Banares by Diana Eck 1993 Boston: Beacon Books

An Open Heart-practicing Compassion by: Dalai Lama 2001 Little Brown and Co, Boston

Faith in Nation: Exclusionary Origins of Nationalism by Anthony W. Marx 2003 Oxford University Press

Britons: Forging the Nation 1707-1837 by Linda Colley 1992 Yale University Press

A Brief History of Everything by Ken Wilber 1996 Shambhala Books

New York Times Article by Alexander Stille 5/31/03

NOTE TO READER:

If you want copies of *Flowers Facing the Sun* for
groups or classroom teaching, we will arrange bulk
discounts. Your input is welcome. Ben B. Boothe

UNICORN PRESS U.S.A.
Fort Worth, Texas

Unicorn Press-USA
9800 Verna Trail N.
Fort Worth, Texas 76116 U.S.A.
benboothe@compuserve.com

ABOUT THE AUTHOR

After graduating from Harding University and a short stint of youth social work, Ben Boothe entered the business world. His experience with the Wall Street investment firm, Merrill Lynch Pierce Fenner and Smith, led him into banking. As an organizer and C.E.O. of several banks, he researched global economic trends and socio-economic impacts of government and financial policy. Through his writings and travels, he was recruited by the USIA/USIS (U.S. State Department) and the World Bank as an international, economic consultant specializing in banking and finance.

Ben has helped several developing nations restructure banking and financial systems during times of crisis. As President of Boothe and Associates, Inc., (a multi-faceted company dealing in valuations, environmental consulting, and international economic consulting) Boothe maintains world wide travel and speaking programs. He has lectured, consulted, and served as guest professor in many venues. One year his schedule took him around the globe three times in speaking for universities, financial symposiums and policy think tanks.

With six books to his credit, he has been featured in hundreds of columns and media interviews in the USA, Europe, Asia and Latin America. He is active in many nations as an incisive observer and adviser of socio-economic trends. His GLOBAL PERSPECTIVES is a bi-monthly summary of trends and socio-economic analysis read by executives and political leaders throughout the world.

Ben and his wife live on a ranch west of Fort Worth, Texas, with 2 dogs, a cat, horses and a mule. They enjoy a steady stream of beloved global generation guests. They summer in a cabin high in the Sangre De Christos Mountains of Northern New Mexico.